Library of
Davidson College

Library of
Davidson College

Guide to Home Language Repair

NCTE Editorial Board: Rafael Castillo, Gail Hawisher, Joyce Kinkead, Charles Moran, Louise W. Phelps, Charles Suhor, Chair, ex officio; Michael Spooner, ex officio

NCTE College Section Committee: Cynthia Selfe, Chair, Michigan Technological University; Pal Belanoff, SUNY–Stony Brook; Lil Brannon, SUNY at Albany; Doris O. Ginn, CCCC Representative, Jackson State University; Jeanette Harris, University of Southern Mississippi; James Hill, Albany State College; Dawn Rodrigues, Colorado State University; Tom Waldrep, University of South Carolina; H. Thomas McCracken, CEE Representative, Youngstown State University; Louise Smith, ex officio, Editor, *College English*, University of Massachusetts at Boston; James E. Davis, Executive Committee Liaison, Ohio University; Miles Myers, NCTE Staff Liaison.

Guide to Home Language Repair

Dennis Baron
University of Illinois at Urbana–Champaign

National Council of Teachers of English
1111 W. Kenyon Road, Urbana, IL 61801-1096

For you, the readers, the teachers, and the radio audience

Illustrations: Dennis Baron
Manuscript Editor: William Tucker
Production Editors: Michelle Sanden Johlas, Michael G. Ryan
Cover Design: Doug Burnett
Interior Book Design: Doug Burnett
Cover Illustration: Dennis Baron

NCTE Stock Number: 19425-3050

© 1994 by the National Council of Teachers of English. All rights reserved. Printed in the United States of America.

It is the policy of NCTE in its journals and other publications to provide a forum for the open discussion of ideas concerning the content and the teaching of English and the language arts. Publicity accorded to any particular point of view does not imply endorsement by the Executive Committee, the Board of Directors, or the membership at large, except in announcements of policy, where such endorsement is clearly specified.

Library of Congress Cataloging-in-Publication Data

Baron, Dennis E.
  Guide to home language repair / Dennis Baron.
    p. cm.
  ISBN 0-8141-1942-5
  1. English language—Usage. I. Title.
PE1460.B376 1994
428—dc20   93-49855
                                                                  CIP

Contents

Preface vii

1. Guide to Home Language Repair 1
2. Admissions Test 13
3. Questions and Answers 22
4. The Language Police 47
5. Teaching English 64
6. The Copy Shop 81
7. Politically Correct Language 95
8. Spelling Counts 112
9. What's the Latest Word? 121
10. Last Words 141

Index 159

Author 165

Preface

I have been thinking about the English language, both seriously and not so seriously, for as long as I can remember. But it was not till about ten years ago that I began receiving requests to talk about my subject, the history of the language and the various attempts that have been made to reform it, on the radio.

I have never enjoyed watching the talking-heads on television: when experts fill the screen, explaining the latest political or cultural crisis, I tune out or take an extended commercial break. And when the talking voices of the radio call-in shows drone on and on in response to questions from listeners, I have trouble paying attention, right as they may be: my mind wanders and my driving becomes erratic.

So I had a little trouble positioning myself when it was my turn to be a talking voice. Until, after a few attempts to take myself very seriously while nobody in the listening audience called in, I decided I could do Aristotelian radio, attempting to combine delight with instruction. And this book, which grows out of my experiences as a radio talking-head, is the result—the closest I will ever come to stand-up comedy.

I would like to thank a number of people who have encouraged me in my madness. David Inge, the host of "Focus 580" at the University of Illinois' WILL-AM, has invited me back as what he calls a "semi-regular guest" (which, it turns out, is not a guest in need of more dietary fiber) for a number of years. In addition, the producers of WILL's "Afternoon Magazine" have aired my "regular" commentaries on the state of the English language for the past four years. Much of the material in this book comes directly from questions that arose as a result of my experience with WILL, as well as from my occasional appearances on a variety of radio shows from New York to Texas to Vancouver.

I also owe a debt of gratitude to the University of Illinois News Bureau. Mare Payne, editor of *Inside Illinois*, found the nineteenth-century university entrance exam (chapter 2) and asked me to answer the questions for her readers. Andrea Lynn, another editor at the News Bureau, has encouraged and publicized my work. My discussion of *factoid* was a response to a question she asked me, and Mark Reutter, also of the U of I News Bureau, managed to place that piece in a couple of newspapers.

I tried out some early versions of the *Guide to Home Language Repair* at Engfest, sponsored by Western Michigan University and the Michigan Association of Teachers of English, and at the spring banquet of the English department faculty of Illinois State University: I'm not sure either group knew what they were letting themselves in for, but I am grateful for their supportive responses.

I would also like to thank Michael Spooner of the National Council of Teachers of English, who encouraged me in the writing of an earlier book, *Declining Grammar,* and who has been equally upbeat as I worked on the present volume, which should really be called *Son of Declining Grammar,* but that is not a politically correct title.

My family, as always, plays a major role in my work, although my son (who is now four) no longer listens to me on the radio because I can't hear what *he* is saying to me into the speakers, and my younger daughter (now nine) did not use my op-ed piece on *factoid* from the *Atlanta Constitution* for her current-events assignment last week because, at 750 words, it was too long.

While many of the words in this book did go out over the airwaves in some form or another, a few also appeared in print. "Entrance Examination" appeared in *Inside Illinois.* The answer to the question "Is there some other way to say *etc.*?" appeared in *American Speech.* The piece on *factoid* appeared in the *Atlanta Constitution* and the *St. Louis Post Dispatch.* And "Dial 1-800-M4MURDR" was first published in *English Today.* All are reprinted with permission.

1 Guide to Home Language Repair

You may well be wondering, What is the *Guide to Home Language Repair?* The answer is simple: It is a book dedicated to the serious language do-it-yourselfer—the teacher, editor, writer, student, or any person with an abiding interest in language and an uncontrollable itch to tinker with it. But don't be fooled: it's no substitute for a usage guide, grammar grinder, or lamentation on the death of language. Truth in packaging compels me to warn you that it does its best to explode the concerns of such books, to get behind, beyond, or beneath them.

The *Guide to Home Language Repair* is a book you can turn to when you have questions about English that transcend "When do you use *can* and when do you use *may?*" Or whether you should use either one. In fact, since one of my fundamental assumptions is that your language probably doesn't need repair in the first place, this book doesn't tell you how to fix your language so much as it suggests ways of coming to terms with language that may trouble you, or give you pause, but that doesn't necessarily need repair. It suggests ways of rethinking and exploring attitudes toward language, ways of accommodating yourself to language trends and issues. It asks you to reconsider your received ideas about language, particularly about how it varies and changes. And it asks you to rethink your preconceptions about language books.

I use the broad and probably misleading term "language repair" because all the subjects I deal with are prompted by questions I get when I do radio shows and talks about the English language. Usually my callers and petitioners want me to fix, condemn, or approve some phenomenon of English, and I often disappoint them by explaining and analyzing the bit of language that's been put on the spot. Instead of agreeing with their gripe, I try to explore the reasons behind their concern.

I also call this subject "home" language repair because I think everyone who has a language (and that includes everyone reading this book and just about everyone that they know) has the ability to work that language themselves—or, if you want to be thoroughly up to date, not to mention outré, themself (but more on the issue of pronoun repair later).

And by the way, although it's a guide to *home* language repair, this book is suitable for apartment dwellers as well.

By now you may be wondering, do you really want to get involved in this business of language fixing yourself? I mean, you gladly pay someone $45 an hour to fix your washing machine, and language is so much more complex than the average home appliance. Isn't this what we pay English teachers for?

We'll get to the business of whether or not teachers should be licensed to repair language in a bit. Even in the best of circumstances, though, you will find you can't get a repair person when you need one, so you'd better be ready to do it yourself. Here a spirit of adventure may be useful, and of course a willingness to get your hands dirty (I do recommend water-based rather than permanent ink, for those among us who are laundry conscious). And don't forget that lots of people cheerfully start a project themselves, and then they call in a pro to clean up the mess they made. If you're that kind of adventurous, then this book is definitely for you.

There are do-it-yourself guides for everything from plumbing and car repair for dummies to job hunting and money management. There are books to tell you how to build a backyard deck and how to get into law school. A few years back there was a do-it-yourself book on how to make an atom bomb. The fact that we're all still here suggests it left out some key step in the formula. One of the latest do-it-yourself books is about suicide, and it's selling like there's no tomorrow. Cookbooks and Dr. Spock are probably the prototypical D-I-Y books, though you could make a good case for the likes of the Bible and the Koran and the Egyptian Book of the Dead as originals in the self-help manual genre (they'd probably call the public TV version of the Bible "This Old Testament").

The *Guide to Home Language Repair* won't tell you what to do with your language, but it will help you get what you want or need out of English. It is designed for the beginner and the expert alike. It's got something for everyone. Whether you've never hefted a pronoun before, or fitted a subject to a verb, or you're a pro used to reading complex sentence diagrams and splitting infinitives safely and efficiently, the *Guide to Home Language Repair* is for you.

You may also be wondering, Who is the author? What are his qualifications? Is he licensed to practice in this state?

I'm an English teacher. When I was younger and brasher, I used to introduce myself at cocktail parties with a glad hand and a silly death-of-a-salesman rhyme: "Baron's the name, English is the game." But now that time's wingèd charioteer has begun to whisper "The game's up" in my ear and the word salesman itself has become sodden with sexist overtones, I just say, "I'm an English teacher."

Trouble is, when I meet people and tell them I'm an English teacher they become embarrassed, look down or away, give a little nervous laugh, and say something on the order of "Gee, er, um, I guess I better watch my grammar." The other day I met a dentist and he asked me what I did and I said, "I teach English." He opened his mouth and said, "Aaah." Then he said, "That was my worst subject." Which put an end to the possibility of conversation. And as he watched his grammar, I could see his fist tightening around the drill.

After ten years of doing radio talk shows about the state of the English language, I've found that getting people to talk about English is a whole lot easier than pulling teeth. The truth is, even if English has been somebody's worst subject, we all like words in general and in particular. And we all have favorite hates, things that make us cringe when we hear them said aloud or see them in print.

Thinking about language is as popular as ever. Language columnists have a devoted and attentive following: readers hang on their every word, waiting for the truth, though they much prefer pointing out the errors.

But while language watching is a popular spectator sport, most Americans—wanting to be correct, but afraid of being corrected—have learned to view language *study* as something to avoid at all cost. So English teachers become as popular as insurance peddlers, shunned by a public that prefers its language shrink-wrapped, tamper-proof, and freshness-dated.

What do I think about all this? Actually, I'm very sympathetic. While I was good at it, language was never my favorite subject in school. My English teachers all expected me to become a scientist. On the other hand, my science teachers knew where my true vocation lay. After I took calculus, my fate was sealed: You didn't have to be a rocket scientist (as the expression goes) to know I was never going to be a rocket scientist. So I became an English teacher. There didn't seem to be any other options. And anyway, it seemed a good deal: I'd be paid to read and write and talk, which are things I would have done for free anyway.

But watching other people's grammar, well, that was something else entirely. Even as an English teacher, I studied literature, not language. I still pepper my conversation with literary allusions, ignoring whenever possible the difference between *shall* and *will* and *can* and *may*. But the people I talk to don't want me to tell them whether Hamlet was really mad or who Shakespeare was addressing in the sonnets. (Or is it *whom?*) They want to know where to put the commas and whether or not to capitalize Mother and President.

The driving need of Americans to be correct in matters of language means I have to answer anxious queries about spelling, punctuation, and usage, telling my petitioners if *whom* is dead and just what the subjunctive is, anyway. And what about that rule for when to use *that* and when to use *which?* Unfortunately, none of *that* makes good radio, and if you've ever looked at an explanation in a grammar or usage book, you know it doesn't make good reading either. So you'll understand if I leave all that stuff out of this book. There are plenty of guides and grammars and handbooks that answer those kinds of questions. They are all very serious and many of them are probably wrong as well, and even if they're not, the explanation they give is so confusing you're bound to make a mistake if you try to follow their advice.

My advice is: Use your ear. If it sounds good, it probably is good. Just like slamming the new car's door in the showroom, you can tell by the sound if you're dealing with a quality product (well, maybe the analogy is not all that great). But you also have to use your audience's ear. I mean if your listener or reader is puzzled, annoyed, or not paying attention, then no matter how good your language sounds to you, it isn't getting across, and everybody's time is being wasted.

Correctness in language is a tricky thing: lots of mistakes are made by people trying to fix something that isn't broken to begin with. I've found that if you just use language instead of worrying about it, you can have fun with words while you build them into sentences and paragraphs and chapters and books. And what if you do break things that aren't already broken as you try to fix them? At least you'll find out along the way just how they would have worked.

Contrary to most people's school experience, correctness in language is not an absolute. Ideas of what is right change, maybe not from day to day but certainly from time to time. Many standard features of Modern English usage and vocabulary were challenged by experts when they first appeared: such common words as *presidential, scientist, physicist, reliable, telegram,* even *ice cream,* were angrily denounced in their day ("approved" alternatives were such barbarities as *presidental, scientialist, physicsist, telegrapheme,* and *iced cream*). Critics claimed *reliable* was wrong, that only *rely-on-able* was correct, but it proved too ugly to live.

And what about the passive voice? It persisted unchallenged for hundreds of years until, in the early part of the twentieth century, it became the bane of teachers and editors, blamed for being an overused, wordy, weak, and deceptive syntactic structure. In George Orwell's essay "Politics and the English Language," first published in 1946 and since taught to generations of American college students, the passive voice is condemned as one of the "swindles and perversions" of English. Yet Orwell himself uses the passive to doom the passive, complaining, "The passive voice is wherever possible used in preference to the active"—that's right, he says "is . . . used," which is a passive construction with a hidden or deceptively deleted agent. Of course, Orwell's real name was Eric Blair. *George Orwell* was a pseudonym. Using a pseudonym is a way of hiding the agent not just of a sentence but of an entire text. What could be more deceptive than that?

Orwell is not alone in committing the sins he inveighs against. So common is this practice that one of Baron's Rules of Usage can be stated (note the intentional passive) as follows:

> When a language critic complains about a word or construction, you can be fairly certain
> 1. that the target expression has already become common enough to be considered standard and correct, and
> 2. that if you read or listen long enough, you will find the offending bit of language in the language critic's speech or writing.

Not only do ideas of correctness change, but the so-called experts frequently disagree about what is good or bad English. One striking example illustrates the absurdity and lexical paralysis that usage controversy can induce. In 1912, two well-respected usage experts hotly disputed the correctness of the phrases *a quarter to* and *a quarter of* in reference to the telling of time. Each expert insisted on a literal interpretation of the phrase, but each came up with a different, conflicting "literal" interpretation. Josephine Turck Baker, the author of *Correct English*, interpreted *a quarter to seven* literally to mean six-fifteen, because *a quarter to* really meant 'one quarter of an hour toward, or in the direction of, on the clock dial.' For her, only *a quarter of seven* was correct, standard English.

But the other expert, Frank Vizetelly, a lexicographer and pronunciation specialist (he later wrote NBC's first radio pronunciation guide), insisted that *a quarter of seven* literally meant 'seven divided by four, or one and three-quarters.' For Vizetelly, only *a quarter to seven* was acceptable. Neither suggested *a quarter till*, presumably because both felt it was a dialect term.

What is the poor English speaker to do in the face of such contradictory "expert" instruction? Better to say *six forty-five* and have done with it, a more appropriate solution anyway now that digital time-telling is fast replacing the analog variety.

In the face of divided opinion on linguistic correctness, we can only conclude that Good English is not the stereotypical fortress defended by a draconic English teacher of uncertain gender and surrounded by a moat of red ink. Correctness is rather more complex than that.

Change is normal, and Good English consists not of a single right answer, but of an ever-shifting set of alternatives that are more or less appropriate, or inappropriate, depending on circumstances. As

Edmund Spenser suggested in the seventh Canto of the *Faerie Queene*, change is the only constant (sorry, it's that literary training showing off again).

Of course, change may happen more quickly in what my students like to call "this busy, fast-paced modern world of today" than it did in the Renaissance, when Spenser wrote. What bothers us most about change is that it creeps up on us unawares. All of a sudden something is different, and everybody else seems to know about it but me. I get the eerie feeling I must have been absent the day it was discussed.

For example, I remember that when I was young there were 48 states and 48 chromosomes. Now there are 50 states and 46 chromosomes. When did this happen? Why didn't somebody say something? Sometimes I think I've been absent most of my life.

And there have been changes in English as well. Only a couple of centuries ago there were 24 letters in the alphabet, now there are 26. (In case you were absent, the "new" letters were *j* and *v*, which actually did exist but were lumped together with *i* and *u* down through the eighteenth century, until they were finally given spaces of their own in the dictionary. Imagine "Sesame Street" with only 24 letters in the alphabet: they'd have to redo more than half the episodes.) And language change marches on. Overnight (I'm not sure which night, since I was obviously asleep at the time), the word *junta* switched its official pronunciation from "hunta" to "junta." The stress in *kilometer* shifted from the second syllable to the first without anyone putting a notice in my mailbox. Only a couple of years ago what was once Romania became Rumania (or was it the other way around?). Of course, my grandmother, who came from there, always spelled it Roumania, but apparently that spelling isn't modern enough any more (more on this later, as well). *Humongous* is a word that took root in our lifetime, as did the new sense of *hopefully* in which the word paraphrases "it is to be hoped" and modifies an entire sentence. Some critics are now complaining that *arguably*, which means "it can be argued that . . ." and which has been around since the late nineteenth century, has suddenly become so widespread it is in danger of being declared a cliché.

But correctness is arguably something important, something to make bets on, something people save up questions about until they meet an English teacher or find a grammar hotline to call. And that's why I find myself on the receiving end of so many correctness questions.

Using This Book

The only tools you'll need for the repairs discussed in this book are those you ordinarily use for reading: light, possibly some eyeglasses, and a pen or pencil, which to me is the most important tool a language repairer can carry.

What? You don't keep a pen handy when you read? Then it's time we changed all that. Reading and writing are so intertwined for me that I feel compelled to annotate everything I read, books, magazines, television listings. I even annotate the *Yellow Pages* when I find an interesting business name, like the Vitale Funeral Home, which suggests a living death, or the even scarier Universal Exterminators, whose service is so lethal that their clients must pay in advance.

If you're a fanatic about keeping your margins clean, or if your reading matter isn't yours to scrawl on, then by all means add a small notebook or pad to your toolchest. By the way, never use a highlighter to mark up a text. Highlighting is a mindless activity; the colors clash with everything, and it's no substitute for your own words.

Some people want a dictionary when they're working on language. It's fine to invest in a good desk dictionary, or even an unabridged, if you're serious about this. But if you're on a tight budget you can really get along without one. You can get the sense of most hard or unfamiliar words from the context. And if you have to ask how to spell a word, then you probably can't afford to use it anyway. Most people have a dictionary about the house, and I suspect most people use their dictionaries for hiding money, pressing flowers, and propping up table legs.

You may wonder, as you read this book, about the absence of diagrams. Surely a D-I-Y book should have some visuals to guide the hapless home language repairer, to show you which is Tab A and where is Slot B. Or how big a 6 × 3/4" pronoun really is (all sizes, by the way, are either nominal or pronominal). And surely a language book wouldn't be complete without (yuck!) sentence diagrams. Well, this one is. And don't worry about which kind of ruler to buy. Language, though it is often iambic or trochaic, is never metric.

Once I got a call from a public television producer who was thinking about doing a sequel to a popular series on the English language. She wanted me to talk to her about a show on usage. She actually said, "Talk to me," just like network execs are supposed to. So I brainstormed for a few minutes about usage, telling her some of the things I just told you, but she interrupted my little lecture and asked me how I would adapt what I was saying for television—"How," and these are her very words—"would [I] make usage *televisual?*" That stopped me. When I asked the producer, "Isn't that what they pay you to do?" she politely hung up. The project never did get off the ground. I've got nothing against TV, but I don't think I can make language televisual, and I also think the printed word is visual enough for our purposes. I guess what I'm trying to say by leaving diagrams out is this: if the words don't tell you, then a picture will be no help at all.

Chances are that if you're reading this book, you've already got some questions stored up you've been waiting for an opportunity to ask. And you may be waiting for me to slip up, too. With luck, I'll answer some of your questions and make the mistakes that make language watching so much fun. And if you still have questions or quibbles with my judgments, write to me care of the publisher and I'll try to address your concerns in the next edition.

And speaking of "This Old Testament," I'll start out the guide to home language repair with a decalogue of general advice, then go on to the specifics. Here are the ten don'ts of English:

The Ten Don'ts of English

1. First off, don't use a sentence that's longer than the tallest person in the room.

2. And number two, which is related, don't try to have a conversation when you are the only person who is speaking. Chances are, the other person isn't listening and, if you go on long enough, he or she may even fall asleep.

   Three (3), repeating yourself is like turning up the thermostat in a crowded lecture hall. Don't say something more than once, even if it's important and there will be a quiz on it later, unless you want your audience to fall asleep.

4. Never believe anything you read about language in the newspaper, and never trust anything you hear about language on the radio (or in a book on language repair).

   The fifth don't—and this is an important one—if you accidentally split an infinitive, don't—I repeat, positively do not—try to quickly fix it with Super Glue. Super Glue bonds instantly to skin, and I've seen so many cases of tied tongues because of sloppy infinitive repair that I would sooner have you end a sentence with a preposition.

   Number six: don't ever use the words *whom, one,* or *grammar.* They are the surest ways to turn off your audience and put an end to useful communication. Of course, if your goal is to put an end to useful communication, you could try asking, "Could you spell that for me?" or telling the person you're talking to that you are an English teacher.

Seven on our hit parade of *do nots:* do not continue writing if the little red "check engine" light comes on on your computer. Take your paragraph immediately to the nearest dealer to determine if you can continue safely to the next chapter.

Eight: don't buy used language. That is definitely a false economy. Brand-new, hot-off-the-press language will last you much longer, and it will be good for the GNP as well. Buying foreign words hurts the balance of trade and increases the national debt. If you must use reconditioned sentence parts, be sure they are installed by a competent professional, and by all means keep your receipt. But first read chapter 6 on plagiarism.

9. Don't ignore the manufacturer's recommendations for maintaining your language: change your vowels every 3,000 words, or every three months, whichever comes first; rotate your adjectives twice a year; and do not exceed four syllables per word for the first 10,000 pages.
10. Finally, if you have a language breakdown when you are away from home, please don't try to find help in the *Yellow Pages.* Local grammar shops may give you a quick fix, but chances are they will only tell you you are wrong, and you'll become unbearably depressed. Much better is the group language-disability insurance being offered by some of the big publishers: they give you 24-hour sentence protection anywhere in the continental United States.

Free Advice

So much for the don'ts. I like to get them out of the way because I'm basically a positive sort of person when it comes to language advice. Here's an example of the kind of thing I will be dealing with.

When you're in the line of work I am, you get a lot of requests for free advice. Now this sort of thing regularly happens to doctors and lawyers and accountants. People come up to them at parties all the time with "What does it mean if it hurts me here?" and "My neighbors are building a fence on my side of the property line. Can they do that?" and "Can I deduct my business-related trip to Disneyworld if it rained the whole time?" Suppose the doctor has had a few drinks—it's a party, after all—and tells you wrong? Is that malpractice? Don't ask me, ask the lawyer.

Anyway, the kinds of questions that I get tend not to be matters of life or death or taxes. They're more on the order of "Is it singular here, or plural?" I'm sitting home one evening trying to battle a few spoonfuls of peaches into my seven-month-old son, when the phone rings; a friend wants free advice. You see, he's writing a book, and his editor wants to make his singulars plurals. Or maybe it was the other way around. I don't remember exactly because by this point I realized I had gotten peaches all over the portable phone, and the baby was shrieking because he'd thrown his spoon on the floor for the hundredth time and nobody was picking it up. So I couldn't hear very well and I was quickly losing the ability to think rationally, if I ever had that ability in the first place.

Well, I don't remember what I told my friend, or if I was right. But he seemed very happy with the advice I gave him, though I don't know how he could have heard it since by that time someone else had given the baby his spoon and he was happily banging it on the tabletop.

A lawyer once told me that free advice is worth what you pay for it, though since the lawyer who gave me that bit of advice didn't charge me I really don't know if it was worth it or not.

In any case, I don't want you to think the advice I dispense in my language books is no good, because you paid for it when you bought the book (or the library did, or your neighbor's cousin). And when I dispense this advice I'm wearing my official Dr. Grammar hat and although you can't see it, the sign on the door says "Ring Bell and Walk In." Assuming you have an appointment and your language insurance card.

Here's another example. I get a lot of questions but don't get much fan mail, so the letter I got the other day was quite an occasion. It was from a retired English teacher and was written with one of those calligraphy pens that makes you want to decipher rather than just read. Anyway, my retired but unretiring correspondent billed himself as "something of a pedant"—which was his way of warning me that I had done something wrong. English teachers can be so subtle (I know, because I am one, remember?).

It seems that in my latest book (*Declining Grammar and Other Essays on the English Vocabulary,* NCTE, 1989) I wrote, on page 125, "There are a number of areas." He felt I should either say "There are many areas" or "There is a number of areas," depending on whether I wanted to emphasize *areas* or *number.* He asked, in conclusion, "Am I wrong?"

At this point there is a rustling of papers and I am heard to say aloud, "May I have the envelope please?" After a pause, then a fanfare, I continue, "Yes, Mr. Retired English Teacher, you *are* something of a pedant, and you are *wrong*. You can say, 'There is a number from one to ten, and I am thinking of it,' but you cannot say 'There is a number of areas' because, luckily for us, we can disregard agreement rules when they conflict with meaning. Furthermore, while *number* may be singular, *a number of* is plural. It means 'several' or 'a few' (it does not mean 'many'). We call this an idiom."

And that, by the way, leads me to my free advice for the day:

When your editor and your retired English teacher gang up to say you're wrong, but you know you're right, though you can't say why, do what the jailhouse grammarians do. Don't throw yourself on the mercy of the language, stand up and plead *idiom*. Being idiomatic is offensive, which we all know is the best defense. "There is not a number of panels of a dozen of your peers throughout the planet who would find for the plaintiff." Which, in unpedantic, idiomatic English, means, no jury in the world will convict you. Case dismissed.

2 Admissions Test

Lots of things in life start off with a test, so I hope you won't mind starting this book with one. We all know that you take tests to get into college. And many readers of this book will have taken SAT or ACT tests to that end, and maybe some of the advanced or professional tests as well. But testing goes back long before the fill-in-the-bubble of the most-nearly-correct answer. Here, for your first test (yes, there are more to come), are the orthography and grammar sections of the admissions test for the Illinois Industrial University (AKA the University of Illinois at Urbana–Champaign, where I have been teaching for some time, though not, as my students assume, since it admitted its first class of students in 1868).

This test, recently dredged up from the University Archives by the folks at the U of I News Bureau, was given around 1871. It is called the "Competive Examination for Prize and Honorary Scholarships in Illinois Industrial University." My News Bureau contact asked me whether the examiners actually might have meant to call the test "competive," since she could find no mention of the word "competive" in her dictionary. I checked around in the *Oxford English Dictionary*, in Webster's *Third* and Random House's *Second,* as well as in American dictionaries published in the 1860s and 1870s, but I drew a blank: *competive,* if it ever appeared anywhere outside the bounds of the IIU, was not common enough for it to have been gathered into dictionaries.

I like to think *competive* wasn't a typo, though. You don't often get printing mistakes on this sort of gruelling exam: if the examiners goof up, what message does that convey to the test takers? Maybe, in the best frontier tradition, the profs at this early prairie college made the word up; or maybe they thought it really was a word. Like it or not, it is a word now. It seems a natural derivative of *compete,* and I rather like it. Use it if you like: if anyone objects, just refer them to me.

Since I didn't really warn you about the test, and since I can't resist, I've taken the liberty of supplying comments and answers, some of which have been updated a bit. According to President Gregory, who was at the helm when this test was first given, you need to score at least 70 percent to be admitted to the U of I. I'd be happy to see your answers, though I can't promise for certain when I'll be able to grade them and get them back to you.

There are actually four sections to the test: orthography, grammar, math, and history. We'll only do the first two. You may start now.

Part I. Orthography:

1. Define orthography.

If you can't define orthography, don't bother with the rest of this section. If you define orthography as 'spelling,' don't expect to get any credit. Even though orthography means spelling, the examiners at the U of I (I'll use its current name) would expect you to parrot the answer that was in the textbook, and that in turn would probably involve answering in a complete sentence. Many nineteenth-century language books were arranged in question-and-answer form, like a catechism, and education consisted largely of memorizing the appropriate responses and delivering them on cue.

According to Samuel S. Greene's popular school text, *English Grammar* (1863), "Orthography teaches the nature and power of letters, and the just method of spelling words." And that's what you would be expected to say to pass this part of the test. Although most people agree that English spelling is madness, we place a high value on correct orthography, and the topic of spelling will come up again and again in this book. Unfortunately, the ability to spell does not correlate highly with the ability to read, write, think, or make high-level management decisions. Usage critics, who had little better to do, argued in the 1870s that since *orthography* literally means correct writing, *bad orthography* was a contradiction in terms and *good orthography* was redundant.

2. How many sounds in the English Language, and how many letters used to express these sounds?

(Note here that there is no verb in this question, which means it is not a complete sentence, but don't bother pointing this out to the examiners, who have long since gone to that great testing center in the sky; if you get them angry and they drop a number-two pencil on you from up there you are in big trouble.)

Greene's *English Grammar* says there are "about forty" sounds in English. Other sources count as many as 44, if by sounds we mean phonemes (a technical term, invented long after this exam was originally given, for the basic sound units of a language). Presently there are 26 letters, and the actual number of "sounds" possible in English is greater than 44 if we count all the different ways people really pronounce the phonemes of English.

3. What is a syllable?

Goold Brown's *Grammar of English Grammars* (1851), a scholarly rather than a popular tome, written by one of the crankiest grammarians of all time, defines a syllable as "one or more letters pronounced in one sound." The *Oxford English Dictionary* gets a bit more technical: a syllable is "a vocal sound or set of sounds uttered with a single effort of articulation and forming a word or an element of a word; each of the elements of spoken language comprising a sound of greater sonority (vowel or vowel-equivalent) with or without one or more sounds of less sonority (consonants or consonant-equivalents)," or their written equivalents.

Neither of these definitions seems to hit the nail on the head. Really, when you think about it, a syllable is the part of a word before which a hyphen goes if it's too long to fit at the end of a line.

4. Give us an example of a primitive and also of a derived word.

Greene says, "A word in no way derived from a *radical* is a *primitive* word." He further defines a radical as "a word or part of a word wholly underived from any other word." Put simply, a primitive is what we call today a free morpheme, a word that cannot be broken up into smaller words or morphemes (a morpheme is a unit of language containing meaning), for example, *test, flunk*. A derived word is one containing a primitive, or stand-alone word, and at least one other meaning unit, for example *testing, flunked, rejection*.

5. In the following sentences capitalize correctly and give the rules:

>new york is the Largest of all american Cities and i heard, but i Understood not.

Correct version: New York is the largest of all American cities. I heard, but I understood not.
Rules: Capitalize proper nouns and the first person singular nominative of the pronoun. I assume the "and" in the example is not really a part of the second sentence. I wonder, too, though not very loudly, why Language is capitalized in question 2.

6. Spell the present participle of the verb "To beg," and give the rule for the spelling.

B-e-g-g-i-n-g.

Rule: The final consonant is doubled before you add *ing* to indicate that the beggar is truly in need, and if I don't get into the U of I my parents will kill me.

7. Spell the plural of "Fly" and give the rule.

The plural of fly is *flies* and the rule is "i before e except after c."

8. Spell and capitalize correctly the following:

a man named john right appeared in vue and was scene buy sevral nabors he bore in his rite hand a peace of potery and a pain of glass to which he had no write.

Correct version: A man named John Right appeared in view and was seen by several neighbors (*appeared in view* implies *seen*; thus, this is redundant). He bore in his right hand a piece of pottery (*potery* may also be a misspelling of *poetry,* which Mr. Right found boring and which was in his right hand) and a pane of glass to which he had no right (if the glass was in his right hand, instead of the pottery or the poetry, then *pain* is probably correct instead of *pane*). A classicist pointed out to me that John Right should really be John Wright. Perhaps that is what the examiners would have wanted, but don't forget, they're the ones who called the test "competive." I prefer calling him Mr. Right.

STOP! Do not go on to Part II until the proctor tells you to.

Scoring guide: 7–8 right, excellent. 5–6 right, fair. 3–4 right, at least you tried. 0–2 right, don't worry, no spelling bee winners ever distinguished themselves in the world of letters anyway.

You may now go on to Part II.

Admissions Test **17**

Part II. Grammar:

1. Decline the pronouns—*He, Who, I.*

As one old Roman, eyeing the barbarians at the gate, said to another, "Let's make like a noun and decline." A normal declination would consist of "No." Or the more courteous, "No, thank you." Of course, you may have guessed that *decline* means something different in grammar. Pronouns are declined as well as nouns. *He* is declined *he, his* (sometimes *his'n*), *him. Who* is declined *who, whose, who(m)*. For two centuries grammarians have pronounced *whom* dead, if they pronounced *whom* at all.

I is declined *I, my, me, mine* (unless you are a monarch or an editor, in which case it becomes *we, our, ours*). Young children, thieves, and the IRS decline *yours* as *mine*.

2. Compare the adjectives—*Bad, Able, Much, Benevolent, Good.*

Students today would assume that compare means they should point out the good and bad qualities of each item, contrasting it with the others in the set. They might give the following answer: "In this busy modern world of today, *bad* is worse than *good*, except of course when it means 'good.' *Able* is very different from *much*, in my limited experience, and I don't think *benevolent* is very relevant."

The grammatical answers produced by a knowledgeable student writing in 1871 are these: *worse, abler, more, more benevolent,* and *better.*

By the way, *much* (comparative *more*, superlative *most*) is related to the Greek *mega*, a new degree-word so far as modern English goes. It fits into the new paradigm, *much, mucho, mega:* "This boom box costs much money, mucho dollars, megabucks." But it is not related to an even newer measure of degree, *big time*, for example, "I studied for this test BIG TIME—Not!" or the even bigger time *majorly*, as in "If I don't pass this and get into the U of I, I'm majorly toast."

3. Give the Synopsis of the verb *Be* through the indicative mood with the pronoun *She.*

If nouns and pronouns are declined, politely and grammatically, to show their different forms, verbs are conjugated. Although synopsis was never a generally accepted grammatical alternative to conjugation, a synopsis of *to be* in the indicative with *she* would look something like this:

She is. Present
She was. Past

She has been. Perfect

She had been. Pluperfect

She shall/will be. First Future

She shall/will have been. Second Future

The fact that these sentences make no sense at all is totally irrelevant to the study of grammar. Children conjugate *give* as *gimme* for all persons.

4. Write sentences containing *That* used as an adjective, a conjunction, and a relative.

Although Noam Chomsky or one of his followers is often credited with creating the ambiguous sentence "Visiting relatives can be a nuisance," the profusion of meanings of *that* is of long standing and generally poses little difficulty, until you have to explain it.

Adjective. That question isn't fair.

Conjunction. That I will fail is certain.

Relative. This is the question that really stumped me.

In addition, *that* can be a demonstrative pronoun and an adverb. Editors often think there is a rule for when to use *which* and when to use *that*, but writers know that they are wrong. And that's that.

5. Define a sentence.

According to Greene, "A sentence is a thought expressed in words." Punctuationwise, as the busy modern student of today might put it, a sentence is the shortest distance between two points. It is sometimes said to be a *complete* thought, though there are any number of complete thoughts that do not seem to be sentences and some sentences have no thought in them at all. Many sentences take longer than they need to to get where they are going. That is because the universe is curved. A sentence may be defined as a group of words containing a finite verb. Perhaps. Or one having a subject and predicate. Oh? But that anticipates the next question.

6. What are the essential elements of a sentence?

Greene says they are the thought and its expression; Brown says every sentence must make complete sense. These grammarians may be colorfully named, but their comments on language are strictly black and white. If we expected every sentence to make complete sense, there'd be very few sentences going about. Brown also says a sentence must contain a nominative and a verb. Other grammarians say that the essentials are the subject and the predicate, both terms borrowed from logic by the Greeks, who invented logic and applied it to grammar. The subject is the thing under discussion; the predicate is what is said about the thing under discussion.

It is a tenet of linguistics that native speakers of a language can divide sentences into these two parts—the subject and predicate—without having any formal knowledge of grammar. However, even this assumption has recently been questioned by researchers who say that the consciousness of subject and predicate is a by-product of the awareness of grammar we acquire when we learn to read and write. According to postmodern literary theory, sentences may not even exist, though we may sometimes sense what was their presence. In contrast, many students seem to think a sentence is defined, "It starts with a capital and ends with a period." And maybe, just maybe, they're right.

7. Define a simple, a complex, and a compound sentence.

Greene says a simple sentence "has but one proposition—no one of its elements being a clause." In other words, a simple sentence is a finite clause which, like the cheese in the nursery rhyme, stands alone. A complex sentence combines such an independent clause with a dependent one, a clause which literally "hangs from" or depends on it by means of a subordinating conjunction. A compound sentence has two or more simple sentences joined at the hip by a coordinating conjunction. And although you didn't ask, a compound complex sentence combines these last (or is it *latter?*) two to form yet another in the endless typology of grammar.

8. Parse the italicized words in the following sentence, and give reasons for each step:

> *Breathes* there a man with soul so dead,
> *Who* never to himself *hath said,*
> *This* is my own, my native *land?*

Breathes: verb, third-person singular indicative interrogative in the present tense.

Who: pronoun relative, of person, in the nominative case, singular, and (sexist) masculine. Or is it *whom?*

hath said: verb, present-perfect indicative, consisting of the third-person singular present (archaic) of *have* plus the past participle of *say,* which today has become *went,* as in, "He went, 'This is my own, my native land,' and I'm like, 'Give me a break,' and then she's all, 'You've got to be kidding.' "

This: demonstrative pronoun, singular.

land: singular noun in the nominative case, predicative of the verb *be.*

The result of this very typical and absolutely meaningless grammatical exercise must have been a complete distaste for poetry, as well as grammar, on the part of students and teachers alike.

9. "I refunded him the money." Change this to the passive construction.

"He was told the check was in the mail."

10. Correct the following sentences when needed, and give the reasons.

1. Which do you like best, bread or fruit?

Better is better. Which is to say that *best* should be changed to *better,* since the comparative is used for two, the superlative for three or more, or at least that's the rule, though many (or is it *most?*) do not follow it. Note that neither bread nor fruit contains much in the way of the four major food groups essential to the health of the undergraduate: sugar, salt, fat, and caffeine.

2. It was him who I saw.

It was he who? It was him whom? It was he whom? Although the last (not the latter!) is most correct, wouldn't it just be better to say "I saw him"?

3. Turn your toes out, like I do.

This sentence is correct. Ever since "Winston tastes good, like a cigarette should," grammarians have fought usage critics for the right to say *like* instead of *as.* Like them, I'd rather fight than switch. Which is what you should be prepared to do if you walk with your toes out.

4. He is an uneasy person; he cannot lay still or set still a moment.

"He is hyperactive."

5. The wisdom and justness of his decisions is now apparent.

Should *is* be changed to *are?* While most examiners would consider this a clear error in subject-verb agreement, the hyperactive student might argue that *wisdom* and *justness* seem to be rolled into a single concept here, like "truth, justice, and the American way," and therefore take the singular form of the verb. What would really make for a trick question is if *decisions* had been singular. Most people are influenced by the noun closest to the verb, so *decision* would trigger *is.* Marketing majors know this fact even before they are admitted to the university.

Scoring your response: 9–10 right exempts you from freshman composition; but if your friends start to call you a grammarian, beware, it's not a compliment. 7 or more right means you're U of I material. 4–6 right, thank you for your interest, we'll get back to you. 0–3 right, you might try one of those schools that advertise on matchbook covers.

3 Questions and Answers

I always insist that it's better to be specific than general, so I'd better get down to the business of answering your questions on language repair.

Sometimes when I open my mail or when I do radio call-in shows under my stage name "Dr. Grammar," I get some pretty strange questions, questions I have no idea how to respond to. Once a caller asked me to condemn the common-enough expression, "Keep off the grass."

"Why?" I wanted to know. "Because it's wrong," he insisted. "What's wrong with it?" I asked. That's what he wanted me to explain. Nothing was wrong with it, nothing could be wrong with it, and even if there were, why would anyone bother to torment such a time-honored phrase? But the caller persisted in his demand that I eradicate—which literally means 'uproot'—this idiomatic weed from lawns everywhere.

Usually my callers know what they think the correct answer is. They're just waiting for me to guess it. Unable to guess this one, I finally asked, "Well, what would you say instead of 'Keep off the grass'?" No luck this time: he had no idea. He figured, after all, *I* was the expert, *I* should know.

If I'd been doing shock radio I could have said at this point, "No, you [insert a strong descriptive epithet here—something like *neogrammarian*], you're wrong, I'm right, too bad," dramatically punched a button on the control board, and gone on in a self-righteous huff to the next call.

But this was a family show on polite public radio, where the callers are the sponsors, so I had to indicate, in my most restrained and neutral fashion, that if there was nothing obviously wrong with the phrase, if it served a clear and useful communicative purpose, and if no suitable alternative could be found, then it wasn't wrong, even if the caller didn't like it, and certainly I couldn't possibly condemn it. That's how you tell someone off on public radio. Then you ask them for a pledge.

I'm sure the caller, who got the satisfaction of hanging up on me, continues to this day to believe that "Keep off the grass" is one of the major "swindles and perversions," to echo Orwell, of the English language.

"I'm sorry Ma'am, but your sonnet won't scan. I'll have to get a price check."

Another caller once asked me about the *less/fewer* rule. Normally, I refuse to discuss this sort of thing on the air. But the question reminded me of an assault I once witnessed at the express lane in a supermarket. Express lanes usually are marked by signs which further explain, "Ten items or less. No checks." In this case, a store servicing an academic neighborhood, a language vigilante had obliterated *less* and scrawled the corrective *fewer* in its place. So there.

It happens that the rule in question, that *less* refers to degree and *fewer* to quantity, was invented in 1770 by a language commentator who took it upon himself to differentiate the senses of two words which had always been interchangeable. It just seemed to him a good idea at the time, and it was logical to think that one word should have one, and only one, meaning. Trouble is, it doesn't work. Few English words mean one thing only, and synonyms abound: that's why English has so many more words than other languages. In this case, *less* has always referred to quantity as well as degree, and it continues to do so in defiance of the eighteenth-century restriction, which was copied by generations of critics who never bothered to examine actual usage. Does a book cost less or fewer than $20? Is a child less than five years old or fewer? Have I made my point, more or less? The true problem with the express lane sign is not the use of *less* but the blatant and unconscionable misuse of *express,* since, in my experience, these lanes are invariably the slowest in the store.

And yet another caller asked how *Romania* is really spelled. Place names change all the time. It was not that long ago that Beijing was Peking, and before that, Pekin or Peiping (the city in Illinois named after the Chinese capital remains Pekin, as does the insurance company based there). Romania with an *o* comes from Late Latin and originally meant the whole Roman Empire. Then the word's meaning shifted to the much smaller area which preceded modern-day Romania, which was initially a Roman province. The first English references to the nineteenth-century kingdom of Romania spell the name of the country and its language with an *ou*. The English spelling then changed to *Rumania* with a *u*.

The Romanians spell their country's name with an *o*. But that did not prove popular with the English, who had a prejudice against the *o* spelling: *Romany* in English means *Gypsy,* always a negative term. The word *Gypsy,* in turn, is short for *Egyptian,* because the English thought the Gypsies came from Egypt, when actually they were from India.

So why the *o* now? Since Romania emerged from the evil empire to join the capitalists, they've begun exporting *o's* to the West (it's one of the few things plentiful enough in Romania to export). Apparently there's now a surplus of letters, because the overthrown regime did all it could to suppress free speech, literature, and the arts. Or maybe we think we're supporting the revolution by exchanging the English for the Romanian spelling of the country's name. Anyway, *o's* seem to be what the West is willing to trade hard currency for. The Associated Press and the *New York Times* have become their first customers. It won't be long before the dictionaries follow suit.

In twenty years, American kids who are in junior high today may look back and say, "I remember when they changed the spelling of Romania," with the same nostalgia I feel when I think of those forty-eight chromosomes and states. Who knows how many letters there will be in the English alphabet by then? Still, I'm sure of one thing: some people will always think there are too many, while others will insist there aren't enough.

But enough preamble. In this section of the *Guide to Home Language Repair* we'll look at some of the questions about language I've been asked when I do my "Dr. Grammar" radio shows (some of which have been on commercial stations, where I had to be even more polite), and the answers I gave, or at least the ones I wish I had given at the time.

Question: My English teacher always told me pictures were hung, people were hanged. Is this still true?

Dr. Grammar: Not any more. Most states go in for death by lethal injection, although electrocution is popular and a good gassing is nothing to sniff at. Actually, according to the latest dictionaries, outside of legal terminology more people are hung than hanged, and of course more pictures are hung than people, which, it turns out, is neither cruel nor unusual but something we want to be proud of.

Question: Is it better to say "I was drowned" or "I drowned"? [Honest, these are real questions from real people!]

Dr. Grammar: Continuing our discussion of the grammatically correct way to die, if you drown, I don't think you can say either. If you're talking about someone else drowning, then choose the active voice only if the person cooperated actively in his or her own drowning. In any case, it is always more appropriate for non-swimmers to avoid water rather than worry about their grammar.

Question: Are lawyers controlling the language, and is there anything we can do about it?

Dr. Grammar: Since I didn't get a bill along with the question, I'll assume the questioner is not a lawyer. In any case, my answers are "Yes, they are." And, "No, there isn't." If you want more information, I'll be glad to send you an estimate.

Question: I can't use *anymore* without an accompanying negative, as in "So many people are wrong anymore." Is something wrong?

Dr. Grammar: No, nothing is wrong, I can't use it either. But I don't recommend consulting a lawyer, even if you feel litigious when other people say it. Language law is still in its infancy, and besides, so many people sue each other anymore that there isn't much either you or your lawyer can do about it. Or is it so many people sue one another anymore?

Question: Is *all right* one word or two?

Dr. Grammar: Those who are certain about things linguistic will tell you that it can only be two words. But for some reason, probably the influence of *already,* with which it is frequently associated in an idiom actually pronounced more like *arite areddy,* lots of people write *alright* in sentences like "Alright, let's go" and *all right* in "These answers are all right." I've even had students tell me their English teachers taught them there were two *all rights,* and presented them with elaborate but not very memorable explanations of when to use which. Those who insist the one-word *alright* does not exist are quick to attack those who use it, not realizing the irony inherent in denying the existence of something that bothers them so much they must attack it. Dictionaries tend to take the more cautious way out by recognizing the occurrence of the variant form and labelling it as incorrect. I predict that *alright* will continue to spread, and that it will continue to be attacked even after it begins to be considered standard English. But I wouldn't be caught dead using it.

Question: I know that language changes from generation to generation. When I grew up a *pot* was something you cooked things in. Now it's something you smoke. And *gay* doesn't mean the same thing anymore, either. I think the language of young people is causing the generation gap.

Dr. Grammar: Pot has been a term for marijuana since the 1930s, if not earlier, so unless you are well over seventy you can't complain that the younger generation has changed meanings on you. In fact, it probably was the questioner's generation that named the weed *pot* in the first place. It certainly was the older generation that invented the term *generation gap,* which became popular in the 1960s. As for what has always been for most people the primary meaning of the word *pot,* I may be mistaken, but I believe you can still cook things in a pot, and poor people are still referred to as potless, though for a different reason.

So far as *gay* is concerned, it has indeed developed a new sense, 'homosexual,' which some people feel is obliterating its older sense, or at least contaminating it. For certain words, their earlier and later senses may continue to coexist—*hectic* can still mean 'feverish' as well as the more common 'very busy,' and *journal* can still refer to daily writing as well as to less frequent publication. But *deer* no longer means 'animal,' and *liquor*, which once meant anything drinkable, is now limited to alcoholic beverages.

Though it has developed a new meaning, *gay* has had a sexual connotation for several hundred years now. In the seventeenth century, a *gay woman* was a prostitute, a *gay man*, a womanizer. According to Merriam-Webster, the traditional meaning of *gay*, 'merry, happy,' persists unchanged: in most cases, there is very little confusion over which sense of the word is intended. On the other hand, the editors at the *Oxford English Dictionary* agree with my caller that the homosexual *gay* is driving out other meanings. So much for consulting the experts. Whatever the eventual disposition of the word, accusing homosexuals of linguistic degeneration seems rather extreme and not particularly to the point. To paraphrase a T-shirt popular among the younger generation: Change Happens.

Question: Does language change result in a loss of precision? Look at the word *parenting*, for example, and the confusion of *farther* and *further.*

Dr. Grammar: If you want to be precise, the answer is *no*. If you want to know why, you have to give a little on your demand for precision. *Farther* and *further*, which are etymologically identical, have always been interchanged in English and will continue to be so as long as I have anything to say about it.

Remember what I said earlier about *less* and *fewer*? It's the same situation here: two often interchangeable words that weren't "broke," but which someone decided to fix. In 1906, a usage critic proposed that we differentiate the two derivatives of *far* by limiting *farther* to distance and *further* to degree. But nobody listens to usage critics, except maybe other usage critics, and while usage critics have repeated this new "law" ever since an academy of one adopted it, most other users of English continue to think it is going too far for one individual to impose such a restriction on everyone else.

The same goes, by the way, for the *that/which* law and the *shall/will* one. But I won't bore you with the details.

As for *parenting*, it has been around since the sixteenth century, though it was rare until the present. Maybe it has acquired the trappings of pop psychology, but isn't it a rather precise way of designating what mothers and fathers do, without carrying the baggage of connotation that surrounds the words *mothering* and *fathering?*

Question: What's the difference between *who* and *whom?*

Dr. Grammar: I've often wondered about this myself. Some people think there's no difference at all. They use *who* even when it's an object, as in the name of a television show hosted by Johnny Carson in the early days of his career, "Who Do You Trust?" Nobody would watch a television show whose title began with *whom,* not even on public television.

The use of *who* for *whom* happens most frequently when the question pronoun appears at the beginning of a sentence. It is seldom found after a preposition, as in

"To who should I send this check?"

(besides, if you're offering someone money, they won't care if you use *who* or *whom*). And it is not a new phenomenon. For over two hundred years observers have claimed that *whom* is dead. But other people insist on keeping *whom* alive, using it even when they should be using *who:* for example, this line from Shakespeare's *Tempest,*

"Young Ferdinand, whom they suppose is drowned."

In any case, reports of the death of *whom* seem premature.

If you want my advice, forget about *who* and *whom* and get on to an important question, like the next one.

Question: You say *like* all the time when you mean *such as.* How can I trust you if you're wrong all the time.

Dr. Grammar: The answer, I suppose, is that you can't. But Emily Post uses *like* for *such as,* and so do a number of prominent usage critics (I always turn to the critics for support when they agree with me). I say *whom* sometimes, and I use *phenomenon* and *criterion* for the singular of *phenomena* and *criteria.* But I don't usually treat *data* as plural and I always use *agenda* as a singular. (The Latin singular is *agendum,* in case you were wondering, but I always call a meeting schedule with only one item on it an agenda.) So if you want consistency, you've asked the wrong language person. And the wrong language. English is not consistent. No language is, not even Latin. Language has patterns, it has standards, it has grammar. But it also has exceptions and variations and life. And a mind of its own that seems to resist whatever direction we try to steer it in. But that's what makes horse racing, and that's what makes language. As far as not trusting me goes, I feel the very same way. It's like Groucho Marx's joke about not wanting to join any club that was willing to accept him as a member. I'd never believe anything I heard from a language expert, and I trust very little of what I read in print, especially if I know I wrote it.

Question: Could you comment on the proper use of clichés? I heard somebody on the radio say "Screech me to a halt."

Dr. Grammar: Some people would say that clichés can never be used correctly, but I think they serve a useful function. So long as we define clichés as 'overused terms,' you can never have too many. Your example, "Screech me to a halt," sounds like it was influenced by another cliché, "Gag me with a spoon." But the question raises an important issue: if we permit clichés, then shouldn't we insist they be used correctly, such as "I screeched to a halt"? And that brings up the added philosophical question, reminiscent of the one about the tree falling in the forest: if a cliché is not used correctly, is it no longer a cliché? "Screeching to a halt" is dull because it is traditional. We don't pay it much mind; we tend not to hear the squeal of the brakes. But *screech me to a halt* is colorful, unusual, definitely noisy. I like it. I just wouldn't overuse it.

Question: I don't like this newfangled use of *hard* for *difficult*.

Dr. Grammar: Good for you, but what's not to like? *Hard* has meant 'hard' in the physical sense (like a rock) since the tenth century. It has meant 'difficult' since the fourteenth. If a meaning that has been in use for six hundred years is newfangled to you, then by all means continue to use *difficult*, which did not enter English until the sixteenth century, making it considerably more newfangled than the oldfangled form you are resisting.

Question: I can't stand it when people say, "Hi, how are you?" "I'm fine, how are you?" "Just great. Well, have a nice day." I mean, really, these things just don't mean anything, do they? People don't want to know how I really am. I could be going off to be shot and they'd still say, "Hey, have a good one."

Dr. Grammar: I'm no fan of "Have a nice day" and its offshoots either, but I do think you're wrong to expect people to use greetings sincerely. When people say, "Hi, how are you?" they usually don't want to know the truth. And when they say good-bye, they're not usually saying "God be with you," which is what *good-bye* once meant. Greetings occur frequently and formulaically. Information theory has it that frequency of occurrence is inversely proportional to information content. Which is the technical way of saying that the more something is heard on the rialto, the less it means. Greetings are about as close as any statement can come to being totally devoid of semantic content.

This is not to deny them an important function: they signal that conversation may begin, or that it is at an end. We use them as empty phrases almost of necessity. "Hi, how are you?" more and more often prompts the response, "Hi, how are you?"—there is no answer, merely another question that is not really a question.

If you respond to "How are you?" with a detailed description of your angst, your aches and pains, news of your dead cat or your recent mugging (in which you were the muggee), you are violating an important politeness constraint on greetings that they not be taken literally. Like as not your interlocutor will squirm to get out of the conversation and on with his or her own life.

Now here's the catch: when a medical person asks, upon walking into the examination room, "Hi, how are you?" you are presented with a dilemma. Do you violate the normal conversational expectation if you launch directly into your symptoms ("Doctor, it hurts me here.")? Or is it a violation to be polite and engage in the conversation-opening ritual of our society, thus wasting the doctor's time? After all, if you talked less he or she could be seeing more patients, playing more golf, calling more brokers. The medics have us over a barrel when it comes to greetings, which is hardly news, since much traditional medical communication is based on putting the patient in an inferior or uncomfortable role. Which is, of course, what *patient* means literally.

Question: I don't like a lot of the words computers are bringing to English, like *slave printer* and *cannibalize,* because they sound so negative.

Dr. Grammar: Maybe computer words are negative because computers themselves are hard, by which I mean difficult rather than resistant to the touch. I suppose one consolation is that it's better to use these terms in a figurative sense as computerese does than in the more literal human senses that gave rise to them in the first place. I hope I never have to eat my words.

Question: When do I say "I feel bad" and when do I say "I feel badly"?

Dr. Grammar: To find that out, I'd have to commit you for observation. But if you are asking for a direction rather than a tally, I will tell you that usage is pretty evenly divided on this pair. This question is a great example of how grammar can get very technical while bearing no relation to actual usage.

In the ninth grade I was told the following, which I remember very well because we were all afraid of the English teacher and also because it was on the test. *Feel* is one of those verbs we call *copulative*, a term we snickered at in ninth grade, which also helped me remember it, and one which I would be surprised to find in an English curriculum today. (And yes, we snickered over the copulative *feel* even more than over the other copulative verbs.)

In any case, a copulative verb takes predicate nouns and adjectives. So if you *feel bad*, meaning you're feeling down, morose, sorry, or not good emotionally, then you say something like "I feel bad Jenny got a raise and I didn't." If you "feel badly," that literally means your sense of touch is not operating correctly, for example, "I feel badly since that terrorist sliced off my fingertips." Or so I was told.

Unfortunately, people don't always observe these niceties, even people who had my ninth-grade English teacher, and so you also hear a lot of "I feel badly about Bill's flunking his prelims." There may be a tendency for people to use *feel badly* when they are talking about an emotional state rather than a physical one, and it has also been suggested that some people avoid *feel bad* because *bad* suggests evil: one nineteenth-century usage guide actually prescribes *feel badly*, saying to *feel bad* is wrong because it means to feel malevolent. So the authorities are divided on this usage issue, as they are on most.

Generally, people have only a dim grasp of the grammar that is supposedly involved in the construction, which strongly suggests that the grammatical explanation crammed into me in junior high school is a phoney one, concocted after the fact to shore up someone's irrational preference for *bad* over *badly*. In practice, both alternatives are right, or wrong, depending on who(m) you ask. So while I feel bad(ly) that I can't give you an unequivocal answer to how you're feeling, I feel good (not *well*) that opinions on the question are so evenly divided that a conclusion is unreachable. Of course I myself can never feel badly, because I had *feel bad* drilled into me by Mrs. B in junior high.

Question: Can you end a sentence with a preposition?

Dr. Grammar: The answer is yes. (In case you just want to know the answer expected on the test. You may go ahead and skip to the next question. Otherwise, you may continue reading.)

The other day I was talking to a member of the clergy, an educated man used to the demands of both writing and public speaking.

He's the kind of person who saves up his language concerns until he sees me. His question was one of the three I am asked repeatedly, "Can you end a sentence with a preposition?" (The other two concern the difference between *that* and *which*, which I regularly refuse to explain, and the proper use of *whom*, which you will notice I regularly ignore since I write for a family audience.)

Now, if I'd wanted to be cruel, I would have said to the rabbi, "Of course, you *can* end a sentence with a preposition, but you mean *may*. *Can* signifies possibility, *may*, permission." But I find it's not a good idea to take that tone with the clergy, because they have friends in high places. Besides, I use *can* and *may* interchangeably all the time; doesn't everybody?

Now back to the question: *Can you end a sentence with a preposition?* It's a perfectly valid question, of course, one which I have been asked several times by people so concerned with correctness in usage that they don't trust their instincts. The answer, as I have already indicated, is yes, you can, you may, and, in many cases, you must.

Prepositions are little words that link nouns or phrases with the rest of a sentence, often showing direction or some other sort of physical, temporal, or logical relation. *Of, for, to, above, over, from, with,* and so on. Purists used to insist that the word *preposition* means 'put in front of' (which, of course, it does, literally), because in Latin the preposition must be put in front of a noun or phrase functioning as its object. That is also true in English, for example, *Althea looked down the street,* where *down* is a preposition and *street* is its object. You can't say, *Althea looked the street down.* On the other hand, you must place the preposition at the end in a sentence like *What are you hitting me for?* You can't say *For what are you hitting me?* without sounding a bit German. Similarly, you must say, "Her suggestions were easy to comment on," "The bed had not been slept in," and "The price wasn't worth arguing about."

However, there are some writers who insist that when you have a choice, it is better not to end your sentence with a preposition. They prefer "I don't remember the name of the drug to which he was addicted," not "I don't remember the name of the drug he was addicted to." Clearly, though, revising your final prepositions so that they are buried in mid-sentence can lead to clumsy, convoluted syntax, or to sentences that are overly formal.

Henry Fowler, whose *Dictionary of Modern English Usage* is the bible, or at least the Old Testament, of usage commentaries, considers the flexibility of placement of the English preposition an asset. According to Fowler, the sentence "That depends on what they are cut with" is not improved by changing it to "That depends on with what they are cut" or the even more absurd "That depends on the answer to the question as to with what they are cut."

Furthermore, even if you cleave to the principle that prepositions go first, insisting that other people avoid final prepositions constitutes an insulting invasion of privacy. There is a story that Winston Churchill, well-known for his ability with the monarch's English, was once corrected by a reporter for ending a sentence with a preposition. Churchill is supposed to have replied, "Young man, that is insolence up with which I will not put."

So, after considering all this, what advice did I give my friend and spiritual mentor? The advice those who are perplexed in their usage are least happy to hear: Don't look for a higher law; use your best judgment. I took my text from the Mosaic code, though since the laws of usage are not graven in stone, I modernized the *Thou shalt nots:* don't follow false rules; don't covet your neighbor's writing; and, above all, don't murder the English language. And I told him that the next time I hear one of his sermons, I'll be listening for his prepositions. It's the least I can do to comfort him.

Question: I can't stand it when people pronounce *etcetera* as "ek-setra." Why do so many people do that?

Dr. Grammar: There are a lot of common mispronunciations I hear about: *axe* for *ask, nucular* for *nuclear, asterik* or *asterix* for *asterisk.* And of course *liberry* for *library.* Actually, "aks" and *ask* have alternated ever since Old English, when both were perfectly acceptable ways to inquire. President Jimmy Carter, who had a master's degree in the mysteries of the atom, called his subject nuc-u-lar physics. And a long string of New York mayors went to the liberry after they were defeated and had time to read again. Some dictionaries even note the mispronunciations of *asterisk,* so common have they become, though no one is willing to officially approve of them.

As for *etcetera,* my guess is that the variant pronunciation is partly influenced by the fact that it is not a native English word, but a Latin one. A quick look in a dictionary at words beginning with *et-* (not counting *eth-,* which is an entirely different sound) shows most of them pronounce the *e* as it is sounded in *eternal.* The short *e* words are *etiquette,* which is French, *etch,* which has only one syllable, and *etymology,* where the first syllable is followed by a vowel (and which is often confused with *entomology*—I remember the difference because entomology includes the study of what my grandmother used to call, in her Roumanian-accented English, *ents*).

So, to start out, *etcetera* is an unusual form, though it is used fairly frequently. Also, *etcetera* is one of those words we rarely see spelled out when it is written. Its usual form is the abbreviated *etc.*, just as the usual form of *mister* is *Mr.* Abbreviations which function as independent words frequently take on their own pronunciations. *Mister* is really a variant pronunciation of *master*, just as *Miss* and *Mrs.*, both of which are abbreviations for *mistress*, have developed their own distinct pronunciations.

The abbreviation *Inc.*, short for *incorporated*, is occasionally pronounced "Ink," for example in the phrase *Murder, Inc.* So I propose solving the *etc.* pronunciation dilemma by introducing a new abbreviated pronunciation to match the printed form: "ets" (it rhymes with *bets*, not *eats!*). I'm surprised *ets* hasn't developed already on its own. It would be especially useful when this word is repeated several times, as it often is both in speech and writing, to indicate an unspecified series of items. So the last few words in the sentence "Fenwick likes correcting other people's grammar, pronounciation, spelling, punctuation, etc., etc., etc." would be pronounced "ets, ets, ets." I suppose you could say "eks, eks, eks" as well.

A final note on pronunciation, which, ironically, is often mispronounced as "pronounciation." Old Mrs. B, who appears in my writing from time to time, always made sure we said *February*, giving full voice to both of its *r*'s ("so few days in February, so many *r*'s"). It didn't take me long to notice that despite Mrs. B's firm guidance, Walter Cronkite, who(m) more Americans looked up to than just about anyone else as a model of correct, intelligent speech, closed his nightly newscast for twenty-eight and sometimes twenty-nine nights a year with "And that's the way it is today, Feb-u-ary (1–29), 1958 (or whatever)." So who (not *whom*) am I to say how a word should be pronounced?

Question: Is there some other way to say *etc.*?

Dr. Grammar: Yes, as a matter of fact there is. (OK, you caught me. This is a phoney question I put in just so I can write about something related.)

There's a new and increasingly widespread synonym of *etc.* going around, one that has not yet appeared often enough in print to have an official spelling. It is usually heard as a set of iambically stressed *da's*: da da da da da da da da da da, and is used where formerly we said "blah, blah, blah" or the more formal "and so forth and so on." It is imitative and slangy, reminiscent of the dahs and dits of Morse code, or a spoken version of the suspension dots of print . . . , or a slurring of the expression "and on and on and on." It joins with *la di da, ya da ya da ya da, tum te tum,* and similar phrases in other languages, to indicate empty or trivial speech.

It has no official grammatical name yet. I call it a summative or completive, though William Safire uses the more colorful term *dribble off.* I recently came across this example in Tom Kakonis's novel *Criss Cross* (New York: St. Martin's, 1990, p. 103), where a waitress (waitperson) is speaking of an unpleasant customer: "[He] flags me down and starts in his eggs is runny and his toast is burned and his hash browns cold and it's all *my* fault, if you can swallow that, and he's not gonna pay, da-dit, da-dit, da-dit."

It's too early to tell whether this expression will develop a standardized printed form, or whether it will spread into more formal print environments. But it's something language-change watchers should definitely be on the lookout for.

Question: What is a factoid? I thought it was a little fact, but someone just told me it was a lie.

Dr. Grammar: This is one of those cases where you're both right—a factoid is both a little fact and a little lie. A *factoid* is defined in up-to-date dictionaries as a false, fictitious, phoney bit of puffery presented as if it were a fact, often as a publicity stunt that, through constant repetition, comes to be believed. The word first appears in Norman Mailer's 1973 biography of Marilyn Monroe. Much of Monroe's life was the product of publicists.

Headlines in the supermarket weeklies also tend to be factoids. Despite frequent claims to the contrary, aliens do not have other people's babies, or vice versa. Elvis sightings are factoids. So are secret messages on Beatles records. But, given the right circumstances, these cultural artifacts become, if not true, at least truth-like.

So fulfilling is the self-fulfilling nature of factoids that the word itself has undergone a change in meaning: although dictionaries have not yet caught up with the practice, reporters and publicists, unaware that the word initially referred to disinformation rather than small bits of honest reportage, are now using *factoid* to mean not a media event but its opposite, 'a small fact, a bit of true information.'

By rights, the word *factoid* should suggest something artificial, something that is not what it seems. The suffix *-oid*, which comes from a Greek word meaning 'shape,' indicates an incomplete or imperfect resemblance to whatever is specified by the root of the word. Planetoids are not real planets. Androids are robots, not people.

Humanoids fool no one into thinking they are humans, or at least, in good science fiction, they don't fool anybody for very long. But factoids *are* fooling us into thinking they are facts. Just look at how many people believe that what politicians assert is the truth.

I have to admit that the process of meaning change usually progresses in a direction opposite to the one taken by *factoid*. A speaker pretends that something is so once too often, and the audience eventually comes to see through the pretense. Distrusting speakers is exactly how a word like *factoid* came into being in the first place. A spin doctor tells us something is a fact. Cynics that we are, we recognize it immediately for the factoid that it really is.

But when we are dealing with words that pretend to be what they are not, especially in politics or public relations, we sometimes have to concede that advertising has been known to work. All too often, the hard sell sells, the illusion does overtake the reality, the hot air of the rhetoric blows us away.

With *factoid*, the root of the word is stronger than the suffix: the *fact* quickly takes precedence over the *-oid*. Factoids are no longer accounts of people abducted by UFOs or contorted explanations of how Rose Mary Woods accidentally deleted 18 1/2 minutes of tape, but stories about President Clinton's favorite place for ribs in Little Rock or a note about Richard Nixon's 80th-birthday cake.

What does it all mean? Do we so much want to believe publicity that we need to treat it as news? Have we so fallen under the spell of the spin doctors that their factoids have become our facts? Are our own belief systems so shallow or uncertain that we are willing to accept assertions as truths?

The change in *factoid* probably doesn't signal anything so momentous. All it means is that journalists have needed a word that refers to an interesting but insignificant bit of information for a long time. Fact has no diminutive: there are no little facts, no *factettes*, *factlets*, or *facticles*. So when *factoid* came along they grabbed it, even though it meant the opposite of what they intended it to mean. And that's a fact.

Questions and Answers

Question: Where does the comma go?

Dr. Grammar: After all I've done, when question time rolls around, when the phones light up or the postcards come trickling in, inquiring minds want to know, *Where does the comma go?* There is a persistent feeling out there that punctuation is one of the most important aspects of language use, second perhaps only to spelling. There are even notions floating about that incorrect punctuation can start a war, send the wrong person to the electric chair, or change the course of world history. Such myths are useful to those who insist on teaching punctuation as if it were divine law. Indeed, in the educational institutions of many states, putting two sentences together with a comma is—you should pardon the expression—a capital crime.

But it is certainly not true that punctuation is revealed truth. There are no semicolons in the Mosaic Law. No medieval divines worried about how many angels could stand on a hyphen. Punctuation, like spelling, is nothing more than a convention of language use, an attempt to supply emphasis, to clarify syntax, and to make writing, when read, sound more like speech. As such, it changes from age to age and country to country. Many people find systematic punctuation, like standardized spelling, to be a great convenience. It can be aesthetically pleasing, as well. And it can reveal a good deal about how written and spoken language works. But it doesn't rank at the top of my language hit parade.

It's clear that many people see punctuation a bit hazily. So they throw commas around like they were reseeding bare spots on their lawn. They add apostrophes like salt and they aren't worried about their blood pressure. Usually the apostrophe signals the possessive. It's used as well to indicate contraction. But it's common enough to see the apostrophe used for the plural, as in "Ripe banana's, 29 cents with coupon" (that these "ripe" bananas are often a deep green reinforces the unnecessary apostrophe). It even pops up for verbs ending in -s, for example, the sign I saw at the IGA last week on some discounted hi-sodium hot dogs with a not too optimistic shelf-life: "Out it goe's." How many of the academics reading this have resisted the temptation to riddle titles of their papers with colons? Maybe I should call this section "Go ahead and make my point: Deconstructing punctuation in the post-cold war era."

And maybe that's why the poet Emily Dickinson relied on only one punctuation mark—the dash—to make her point. The pianist Victor Borge underlined the silliness of punctuation by giving sound

"Alright, where does the comma go?"

to exclamation points, commas, periods, and question marks in one of his funniest comic routines.

Adding punctuation to spoken English might help us to perfect punctuation in written usage. Or it might put punctuation in perspective. But comma I don't suppose that we are ready for a punctuation hyphen free society comma or that we even want one period Or even that we apostrophe re ready to relax our guard and permit random punctuation period That would lead to anarchy comma or at least to fewer red marks on English compositions period

Maybe you were waiting through all this for me to tell you where to put that pesky comma, question mark. Well comma I apostrophe m not going to do it comma am I question mark exclamation point. And that apostrophe s final. Period. Period

Question: So, you're not gonna tell me where the comma goes?

Dr. Grammar: Actually, I haven't decided yet. I mean whether to tell you, not where it goes. I admit that people place a lot of value on the humble comma. A colleague of mine tells his students that comma errors on their papers will brand them as illiterate, so if they make any comma errors he will fail them. I don't know how the students feel when they hear this. I imagine they feel illiterate, because they have probably forgotten where to put their commas and since they already sold their copies of *Comma Care and Feeding* back to the used-textbook store (which turns around and sells them as "preread" books, not used ones) it will be difficult for them to find out. Commas are a subject which seems to baffle students as much as quadratic equations or metaphysical chemistry. Yet they are so central to the academic way of life that their misuse is seen to threaten academic culture, the quest for knowledge, truth, justice, and the American way.

Now, I could get picky and say to my colleague, if you think comma errors are prima facie evidence of illiteracy then you are not using *illiterate* correctly to mean 'unable to read and write,' since to use a comma at all requires the ability to write, which in turn presumes the ability to read. Fortunately, I don't say things like that to colleagues, because such a statement is itself incredibly picky and if I said things like that very often I wouldn't have friends.

Why do people get so exercised about punctuation? Maybe misplaced commas can be a matter of literal life or death if you are drafting a law or putting out a contract to have someone rubbed out (I suppose *erased* would be a better term in this context), but most writers never do things whose punctuation will change the course of history. True, punctuation can lead to ambiguity, but there are many things that interfere with communication more seriously than punctuation. Using words like *illiterate* in an extended sense to mean "You don't know as much as I do" is one of them.

But getting back to punctuation, there are really two basic approaches you can use. Some people prefer to avoid it whenever possible, producing a clean, uncluttered page. Others love to salt and pepper their words. They put quotation marks around everything, even their own names—you've seen those pickup trucks with signs like Wolfgang "Bubba" Beethoven or Jesse "I don't know much about art" Helms.

We shouldn't be surprised to find commas popping up where they don't belong, or missing from places where they do. For one thing, the conventions of punctuation have varied over the centuries. In the oldest forms of English the major mark of punctuation was a dot, like the modern period, but placed in the middle of a line of writing, not at the bottom. This dot appears at the ends of sentences.

It marks off sections within sentences, and it is sometimes found in the middle of a word.

The *comma* wasn't even originally a punctuation mark. *Comma* comes from a Greek verb meaning 'to strike, cut,' and it referred initially to a 'cut-off' or section of a sentence somewhere between a phrase and a clause in length. In this sense, a comma is the grammatical equivalent of a yardstick. Similarly, *colon* meant a group of words clustered into a clause, and a *period* was an entire sentence, usually one composed of several clauses artfully linked together. It was only later that *comma, colon,* and *period* came to refer not to groups of words but to their punctuation marks.

Punctuation has become such a hot topic that some people are campaigning to do away with it (the mystery novelist H. R. F. Keating, for example, has called for an end to the apostrophe for some time now), while others are inventing new punctuation marks to confuse us further. Someone has come up with a sign, a combination of question mark and exclamation point rolled into one, to signal a rhetorical question. You know what those are: questions that are asked with no expectation they will be answered? They're really statements rather than questions, and writers often wonder whether ending them with question marks is altogether appropriate. Then there's a mark that's been proposed to signal an ironic comment, when you say something but mean its opposite, like, "Oh, that's really good."

I don't hold out much hope for the success of these innovations, but there is a new punctuation mark that seems to have demonstrated its tenacity: it doesn't yet have a proper name, but most folks call it the "smiley face." Yes, the smiley face started as an isolated icon, a representation of the phrase "Have a nice day." But since it has become increasingly associated with text I now daringly predict that it will soon serve as our newest mark of punctuation. The smiley face is added to informal letters and notes with depressing regularity. Students put them on their papers before they hand them in, hoping that the smiley face will put the teacher in a happy frame of mind when the grading starts. Apparently this works, because smiley faces are regularly drawn or stuck onto students' graded papers by teachers, who seem to have tired of the more traditional stars. Electronic mail junkies use a mark meaning something like "that's a joke" which consists of a sideways smiley face, :-)

I could suggest to my punctuation-conscious colleague that it is time to invent a mark that tells students they are illiterate, perhaps a smiley face with the mouth turned upside down, like the comic-tragic masks of old (for all I know, someone has already thought up the frowny face, and patented it). He could put one alongside each comma fault, and one at the end of the paper as well, to accompany the failing grade. Perhaps the message of the frowny face would also become a new insult phrase in the English language: "Don't have a nice day!"—something to replace those tired old attacks on people's parents. But, since I can't remember what the new irony punctuation sign is supposed to look like, my colleague would probably take me seriously and he would surely think it was a good idea anyway.

In case my message here is ambiguous, let me state it clearly, without further punctuation:

> A punctuation error should not be the sole criterion for failure
>
> I do not think new punctuation marks are in order
>
> I do not really favor the frowny face and I sincerely hope the smiley face goes away

Question: Yes, okay, very funny :-), but, really, aren't you going to tell me—where do I put the comma?

Dr. Grammar: If you really, truly insist on knowing something so devastatingly trivial as where to put the comma, then yes, I suppose I can answer after all. Because, at last, the federal government, long responsible for trivial matters, has taken a stand on the issue. Specifically, the United States Postal Service wants to tell you what you can do with your commas, and all your other bits of useless punctuation, too. You can find this information on the inside front cover of booklets of stamps. It says, "Please use all capital letters with no punctuation in addresses."

How simple it all is once the government steps in. You want to know where to punctuate? The answer is, "Nowhere." If in doubt, don't.

The government, in its infinite wisdom, knows how to do things right. After years of auditing our tax returns, the government also knows that, given half a chance, the public will do things wrong. They've seen what we can do with the apostrophe and the quotation mark. Semicolon fraud, rampant in the lawless thirties, has been all but stamped out. Now our constitutional right to bear commas is under attack, and I hear they're even thinking of replacing the question mark with the Fifth Amendment.

But what does the Postal Service mean when it says "No"? It means no comma between the city and state: if you're writing to New

York New York, that's what you write, or rather, you write not New York comma N period Y period but New York space NY. And use only capital letters so that letter sorters in the post office can read the address more easily. You don't want to irritate the letter sorters or they'll send your punctuated, lower-cased missive off to "NJ" instead of "NY."

To get people to give up their commas and periods, the Postal Service is offering us amnesty: turn your unused punctuation marks in to the nearest post office and the government will melt them down and turn them into new federal regulations.

Although the Postal Service says it wants no punctuation in addresses it turns out that they mean *almost* no punctuation. When you get down to the ZIP code they want you to use the nine-digit version, the so-called ZIP plus four. In the example they give, if you're writing to MR (that's M R, no period) John Q (no period after Q) Mailer (no relation to Norman "Factoid" Mailer) who lives at 300 E (for east, no period) MAIN ST (S T no period) APT (no period) 211 in DULUTH (no comma) MN (for Minnesota), the ZIP is 55803–0034. Repeat, 55803 DASH 0034.

Stop me if I'm wrong, but I thought the dash was a punctuation mark. My *Random House Webster's College Dictionary* says it is. And of course there's the example of Emily Dickinson. But the U.S. (that's U period S period) Postal Service, in its effort to keep down the cost of postage stamps, insists that it is not. Perhaps the Postal Service is following Emily Dickinson's lead. Perhaps they will soon require dashes where once we used commas and periods. For the present, however, punctuation in addresses is a violation of federal regulations and could be punishable by a fine. So, if you've got any questions about where to put your commas, don't ask me. Instead, send them, together with the commas, to the United States Postal Service BOX 449995 KANSAS CITY MO 64144 DASH 9995.

And speaking of commas, which we always seem to get back to, a physician from Paris, Illinois, writes to ask, "What, is the word, that means, the overuse, of commas?"

Dr. Grammar: (without missing a beat) "Commatose."

I thought I thought of it first, but I find that James Thurber used *commatose* in *The Years with Ross*. (I admit that this is one of the rare instances where I did consult colleagues before answering.) There are other candidates for "comma happy." I briefly considered the more technical sounding *virgulitis,* which in its chronic form becomes *virgulosis.* But since the virgule generally denotes a slash as well as a comma, I thought it might cause some confusion. A colleague suggests *polycommaton,* on the model of *asyndeton,* a rhetorical term which refers to the absence of sentence connectors like *and.* Another coins *hypercommonality.* And a third wants me to tell the inquisitive physician to take two asterisks and call me in the vocative.

I wonder, as well, in considering my answer to a physician's language question, whether I am within my rights in sending him a bill? Surely if I consulted the Paris medic about a physical symptom he would charge me what my insurance company euphemistically refers to as a regular and customary fee. But I don't suppose doctors carry language insurance, so I'll just have to write this answer off as *pro bono.*

Finally, I got a letter asking whether you can say something was "very excellent"?

According to my correspondent, who felt compelled to answer his own question, which made me wonder why he bothered to ask it, you cannot. Apparently the whole thing was triggered by a football grudge. I have to admit that I don't follow college football closely at all, but I do know that the University of Illinois played Virginia in a post-season bowl game named after fruit. I know this because a few weeks after the game a letter was passed on to me, as resident grammarian, from an irate Citrus Bowl viewer and University of Virginia fan, crying foul.

No, it wasn't an illegal procedure on the field that prompted this complaint, but an expression in a University of Illinois promotional video aired during half-time. In the clip, a university student commented that the education one received at the big U was "very excellent."

Now, complains our worthy opponent cum correspondent, "the meaning of 'excellent' is 'superior to' or 'surpassing.' It is hardly a candidate for garnishing with 'very.' Yet there it was being garnished on national TV before ardent supporters of the University of Virginia like my daughter and me."

I didn't happen to see the Citrus Bowl, but I do know that our Virginia supporter and his daughter have lost the game on the playing fields of grammar, as the plaintiff chooses to call them. He considers the word *excellent* to be an absolute adjective, one which cannot be compared. I regret to say that he is wrong.

We often hear complaints about the use of words like *perfect* and *unique*. Purists have argued since the dawn of time, or at least since the eighteenth century, that something can only be *perfect*. It cannot be *more perfect* than another thing, because perfection is the best that you can be. Similarly, *unique* means 'one of a kind,' and it is illogical to think of something as *more unique*, or more one-of-a-kind than something else. Of course, language is not always used logically, and it is common to hear "This is the most unique achievement in the world of sports" or "She is the most perfect example of a grammarian that the world has ever known."

Perfect, like most of the so-called uncomparable (that's not quite the same thing as *incomparable*) adjectives on the usage critics' hit lists, has been used in the comparative and superlative since the fourteenth century by standard authors. The preamble of the United States Constitution contains the phrase, "in order to form a more perfect union." Indeed, according to *Webster's Dictionary of English Usage*, most English adjectives are too restricted in meaning or too technical to be compared: can you imagine *more ultraviolet, most diocesan, least incomparable? Extreme* seems to mean something already superlative and therefore uncomparable—to be *in extremis* means you have already been all that you can be, and soon will be no more; yet we commonly think of things as *more* or *less extreme*.

But what about *excellent?* According to the *Oxford English Dictionary*, the first recorded use of *excellent* in English, dating from the fourteenth century, shows the comparative form *more excellent*. Shortly thereafter we find the superlative, *most excellent.* In the seventeenth century it was even considered acceptable to say *excellentest.* As excellent a writer as Shakespeare knew there were degrees of excellence. In the graveyard scene in *Hamlet*—Act V, scene i, if you're counting—the melancholy Dane says, "Alas, poor Yorick! I knew him, Horatio, a fellow of infinite jest, of most excellent fancy."

It is hard to accept defeat, harder still to accept a defeat in the Vitamin C Classic that is absolute, final, extreme and irrevocable. But you shouldn't take out your frustration at losing a little football game on the English language. The odds are that you can't beat English; so you just have to join it. It has, after all, the home court advantage.

Make My Day

Not all the questions on language that I get come over the phone or over the transom. Some of them come from my family. Those tend to

"*That* or *which*? Go ahead, Cooperman, make my day."

be the toughest questions, the ones I'm most likely to answer with "I don't know." It has gotten to the point where these "I don't knows" generate exaggerated groans and reprised choruses of "Doesn't Daddy know anything?"

So when my son, who was about to turn four (purists will note that he was just seven months old when this book began), asked me one day, "What it means, 'Make my day'?" I thought I might finally have a chance to redeem myself, to prove that I did know something, after all. Until I tried to explicate this catch phrase of American English.

My initial mistake was in rejecting the cinematic approach. I decided to skip Clint Eastwood and Dirty Harry. I told Jonathan about how something could make your day if it was so good or so significant that it made you feel you had really accomplished something. He just stared at me. So I tried again, with an account of how one person dares another person to do something so that person A could then do something that would be very satisfying. More stares. After a few more misfires I came to realize I was not making my day.

Finally, Jonathan came to my rescue. He dismissed my explanations with a "No, that's not what it means." Then in a four-year-old's deadpan voice, he delivered the punch line. "Daddy," he said, "you say 'Make my day' just before you kill somebody."

4 The Language Police

Question: Speaking of Dirty Harry and the law, is there a language police? Dr. Grammar: No, but I can't do justice to this question with a brief, flippant answer; it merits a whole, flippant chapter.

There are a lot of vigilante groups and word gangs out there vying for control of the turf. Every language guru from the nineteenth century's Richard Grant White down to today's William Safire has had such a posse backing them up: White called his thugs the "language detective police"; Safire uses the term "linguistic irregulars." Both of these smack of Sherlock Holmes. Safire's word-watching predecessor at the *New York Times*, Theodore Bernstein, coined the term "delinguancy patrol," a phrase that does not trip lightly off the tongue. Luckily this didn't catch on.

What these private language cops do is issue citations for the use of contested forms and write nagging letters to the editor. Constitutionally ungrateful, they set up sting operations attempting to catch their control agent in some blatant and compromising verbosity. They are Guardian Angels, without the red berets, guarding the muggers and mugging the guardians, making the English language safe for the rest of us. Or dangerous, for in their tireless efforts to purify our speech they manage to remind us that language is a minefield for which they have only pieces of the map.

For as long as anyone can remember, the language police have been patrolling the lanes and byways of the English language, bent on trapping miscreants in felonious misdemeanor, committing flagrant delicts against the English language. Of course the verb squad isn't always so flowery (you might have already guessed that in addition to the uniformed tropes there's a plain-speech division). But you will know when they come for you: boots clattering on the stairs in the dead of night, a loud knock on the door. They have no warrants, no habeas corpus will protect you. They are an unrestrained private army, bullying hapless civilians. Like junkyard watchdogs, the language cops growl a lot and never seem to sleep, but they wind up biting their masters and each other while the rest of us slink off in yet another narrow escape. Villains caught in the act may be given frontier justice at the nearest tree, or suffer a long, slow death by the publication of their crimes.

Becoming a member of the language police is easy. There's no special oath or badge or secret decoder ring or quota of arrests. And there's no rule book to enforce, no rules of evidence to follow: just make your own rules and collar offenders at will.

Perhaps you've caught on by now that I think these defenders of the tongue are wasting their breath. I'm not looking to become grammarian general over the idiom infantry. Some people think all teachers are enrolled in the language police at birth. But I think teachers have been given a bum rap. The stereotype of English teacher as language pedant just doesn't hold.

Slapping 'Em Silly

In the summer of 1992 I began hanging out with an unsavory crowd whose avocation is to argue bluntly about the finer points of English usage. They do this facelessly, over computer networks, sending their beliefs into the ether with religious fervor. Predictably, they disagree with one another, and they emerge from the democratic exchange of autocratic ideas convinced that they alone are right and everyone else is wrong. In the process, they shed some light on how attitudes toward language are formed, and how the language police gets its recruits.

Here's an example of what they say: "People who begin sentences with 'And,' 'But,' or 'Or' should be slapped silly by an English teacher."

As an English teacher, I take some umbrage at the assumption that it is the job of English teachers to patrol the language of their students. For one thing, English teachers are no better at behavior modification than psychologists are.

For another, English teachers have very little training in language enforcement. Their course of study consists largely of literature with an overlay of pedagogy. For their teaching license, English teachers may be required in some states to take one course in grammar or linguistics. This hardly makes them experts in the field.

So why, then, do English teachers go around telling their students they can't use *can* but must always use *may*? Because society expects English teachers to be language experts. Teachers are expected to join the language police without so much as a certificate from one of those schools that advertise on your local cable channels. You've seen the ad, I'm sure: "If you can parse this sentence you can qualify for professional pedant school and drive those big rigs."

Fortunately for us, only a few teachers do elect to wear the mantle of linguistic correctness and throw their weight around. This vast minority is the source of the stereotype, the English teacher who slaps students silly, figuratively speaking, for starting sentences with conjunctions. I had one of these teachers in the ninth grade. Maybe you did, too. The kind who made the parts of speech into medieval torture.

The average ninth-grade prisoner of hormones wants to snicker and giggle or blush when the teacher mentions conjugating verbs. Mrs. B's approach to verbs was so clinical our class decided if sex was like grammar, well then, forget about it.

In Mrs. B's class, the law was the law. You did not split infinitives. You did not splice commas. You did not start sentences with *and*, or *or*, or *but*. (Oh, and you did not use contractions.) We didn't, that is, until the day she insisted that *aerial*, another name for the antenna-things that studded the roofs of houses before cable TV, was pronounced a-e-rial (rhymes with *gray cereal*). Which we knew it wasn't, even if dictionaries did list it as an alternate pronunciation. Nobody in New York said a-e-rial. Nobody on TV did, either. Which meant that nobody in California did. So that pretty well covered the whole country, didn't it, not to mention the known civilized world and English 9SP2 at Russell Sage Junior High?

I must have had more than thirty English teachers during my many years in school, and not a single one shared Mrs. B's high-handed approach to language, or her unnatural pronunciation. As an English teacher, I've met hundreds of other English teachers, yet I can count no more than two or three who fit the stereotype of English teacher as grammar goon. Most English teachers are blissfully unaware of the usage controversies swirling over the computer airwaves. They could care less (or they couldn't care less) if you start your sentences with conjunctions or end them with prepositions, so long as your wording is clear and your handwriting legible, and you don't pass notes in class.

But the idea that English teachers can change the course of the English language by slapping students around is ridiculous. If we had any real effect on people's usage, then we'd quickly put ourselves out of business, wouldn't we? There'd be no more prepositions at the ends of sentences, and all those folks on the computer networks would have nothing left to turn their noses up at.

The Maire and the Supah

Of course some teachers have been trying to ban what they regard as lazy speech since schools began. That's because in order to become teachers they have to pass very strict speech tests which were originally designed by the language police to weed out blacks, Jews, Chinese and other "undesirables" from the teaching force. Even if hiring is fairer these days, the speech requirement persists. So the teachers figure if they have to speak so precisely, then their students should as well.

A few years ago, when Ed Koch was still mayor of New York City, he appointed Richard Green as his new superintendent of schools. New York schools already had locked doors, barred windows, and resident police. Green decided he would meet the challenge of student discipline with a two-fisted attack on students' language, starting with the ever popular "Whatcha doin'?" and its inevitable response, "Nuttin'."

The maire and the supah wanted the schoolkids to say, "What are you doing?" and "Nothing," or better yet, "Not anything." They weren't so foolhardy as to suppose the kids might think they were actually doing *something* in school. (How many times do students say to their teachers, "I was absent on Friday. Did we do anything?" I'm always tempted to answer, "No, it was business as usual," but they'd probably think I was serious.)

The maire and the supah also banned "Yup, you betcha," which is to be replaced by "Yes, you're right." I don't know anyone who says "you betcha" in New York anymore. It wasn't even common when I was growing up there way back when the producers of today's nostalgic shows about the 1950s were suffering through the misery that the 1950s really were. But I know the form must be popular with the folks in Minneapolis, where Superintendent Green was head of the public schools before he left for the Big Apple.

Green's language police won't let you leave the room if you say, "Can I leave the room?" Of course, if you say what they wancha to say, which is "May I leave the room?" they won't letcha do that, either. The universal *brang* will be changed to *brought*, and "What youse want?" (which actually sounds more like "Whachyouse wan?") will become "What do you want?" And *axe a question* must be changed to *ask*. Of course, you can't say *ain't* in school. Or should I say, you mayn't say *ain't*?

I hope you're following all this, because there is going to be a test later.

The maire and the supah actually prepared a list of the top twenty "speech demons" in the naked city—and the supah promised to declare a "Putting Your Best Speech Forward Day" to rid New York of the words that have made it famous. I have no idea whether this day actually was observed (Superintendent Green died after only fourteen months in office). "Good Speech Weeks" were popular in American schools earlier in the century, when students were urged to turn in their classmates for breaking the rules of English without a pass from the teacher. Which is another reason grammar has such a bad name today.

Maybe the schools should set up a speech demon hotline, so that students could report one another for using bad language. I mean, if these kids are walking around with pagers and cellular phones anyway, why not put them to some use that is both legal and nonprofitable?

Now here's the speech demon test I promised. Ready?

1. Which is right and which is wrong, *axe a question* or *ask a question*? Hint: we talked about this earlier, but you may (not *can*) have been absent. In your answer, you might also discuss *asterisk* and *asterix*, which we know are both correct because the latter doubles as the name of a French comic book series.

2. Is *youse* singular or plural? (I suppose if you're from the South Bronx, the question should be, is *you all* singular or plural?) Hint: A good test is whether New York cabbies use *youse* in the singular, since taxi drivers in New York have to be licensed by the language police.

3. If Garrison Keillor said "Yup, you betcha" on the streets of Lake Wobegon, would you have him arrested? If you answered "Yup, you betcha," to that, you can spend the rest of the afternoon in the principal's office. Or you may.

Please send your answers to these questions, in twenty-five words or less, by the start of school, to me in care of the publishers. Entries will be judged on neatness, and aptness of thought. In the case of a tie, or even in the case of a clear winner, no prizes will be awarded.

English without Being

You may have heard in the news recently about *E-Prime*, a version of the English language without any of the forms of the verb *to be* that is espoused by some members of the International Society for General Semantics.

General semantics—its very name has a military air—began fighting linguistic imprecision and obfuscation—propaganda, to put it baldly—long before George Orwell began his more celebrated campaign. It originated in the 1930s, the brainchild of a Polish engineer, Count Alfred Korzybski, who argued that language can distort our perceptions of reality. A number of the General's semanticists have insisted that the use of *is, am, are, was, were, being,* and *been* leads to sloppy thinking, deceptive practices, and, of course, the incalculable evil of the passive voice.

According to the linguist Geoffrey Nunberg, throughout its history, general semantics has remained faddish and well outside mainstream linguistics. Speakers of English Prime, what you could call "English without Being," represent a fad within a fad, closer still to that lunatic fringe of language reformers who want to simplify our spelling, recast our pronouns, expel foreign words from the language, or abolish the apostrophe. E-Primers claim to have internalized their is-less English so efficiently that they can speak and write for long stretches without once resorting to the offensive little verb that the rest of us find so essential. And it is essential. Forms of the verb *to be* are the second most frequently used elements of the English vocabulary (the article *the* is the most common). And, historically speaking, *to be* is an old, honorable, native English word, while *the* is a newcomer, borrowed by English from Old Norse.

By the way, the words *essence* and *essential* come from Latin *esse,* which means 'to be.' I wonder whether they are banned from E-Prime as well? Or what E-Primers find so inimical in the use of *to be* in such essential forms as the progressive aspect: "We *were* going to mug a semanticist, but we changed our minds"? Or the perfective, for example, "Sally has *been* avoiding verbs most of her life"? The passive voice is a syntactic structure often blamed for hiding blame. But here, as elsewhere, the speaker, not the language, is at fault. And it is certainly not the fault of poor *to be,* the passive auxiliary. Moreover, *get* has taken over many of the functions of *to be* in the passive, for instance, "Pat really *got* stung by that insider trading scam," so dropping your *be's* isn't going to take much of the sting out of the passive.

Even so, the troops of General Semantics complain that *to be* makes things too neat, too permanent, too true. For them, saying "A *is* B" prevents us from considering that A may also be D or E, or even B minus. But that's not philosophical rigor, it's just plain silly. We don't interpret statements like "Mel drinks tea" as precluding Mel's drinking or even eating anything else, or performing acts other than ingestion, like breathing or thinking or deciding for herself whether or not to use a verb. (OK, I tricked you—you probably assumed Mel was a man until you tripped over the pronoun. Language does predispose us to think in certain patterns. But it does not prevent us from breaking out of those patterns, either.)

E-Prime may seem just like a word game when you hear about it. Like seeing how long a story you can write without using words that have the letter "e" (*e*-less novels, or lipograms, have been written in several languages, though why anyone would bother is beyond me). But when you turn E-Prime into a program for human improvement it becomes pernicious. I've seen a number of students who have been told by their English teachers that they couldn't use *to be* in their writing. None of them remembered *why* they were told not to do it. But they obeyed, blindly and awkwardly because, like good soldiers, or good students, they knew that orders is orders, which E-primers must paraphrase as "orders exist as neither more nor less than orders, and therefore you cannot contravene them," hardly a precise or imaginative alternative. And when their next teacher told them to use *to be* whenever they needed to, they became confused but dutifully tried to bring the *b*-word back from exile.

What makes for misused language in this case is not the vocabulary of English but an educational system where students are rewarded for doing what teachers tell them to, no matter how misguided or inconsistent, and where they are punished for striking out on their own.

In response to Hamlet's soul-searching question, "To be or not to be," speakers of E-Prime choose not to be. Of course, if you think that dropping a verb will put you in tune with the universe, hey, I'm not going to stand in your way. Hamlet chose *to be*, but he wound up dead. It's gonna happen to all of us sooner or later, no matter how we conjugate our verbs.

The Education Police

Ever wonder what would happen if the language police were really armed? Maybe that's not so far-fetched as it sounds. On July 5th,

"You have the right to remain silent."

1990, the *Chronicle of Higher Education* reported that the U.S. Department of Education "asked Congress for permission to provide [its] employees with guns to protect themselves while enforcing department regulations" ("Ways and Means," A19). Of course, students have been bringing all sorts of weapons to school for years, but now it seems the guardians and transmitters of our language and culture, the Department of Education police, will finally get some muscle to defend us from ourselves. Although the employees in question are charged with pursuing criminals suspected of defrauding the DOE of funds, the idea of armed Education Department workers prompts me to speculate just how these gun-toting Literacy Rambos might operate in our schools and colleges.

First the uniform. The Ed Cops will be decked out in mortar boards and mirrored bifocals (with UV screen, naturally). Those with Ph.D.'s, like former Education Secretary, later Drug Czar, William "Wild Bill" Bennett, will carry the rank of sergeant (*honoris causa*) and wear three stripes on the sleeves of their Kevlar-lined academic robes. The new federales will drive AMC Pacers, specially equipped with high-powered reference books with microscopic sights, from which they can flag down students for incorrectly displayed commas, cite instructors for digression, and hale deans into court for administrative oversight.

Remember Sgt. Joe Friday's "Just the facts, ma'am, just the facts"? Well, the dreaded Ed Cops, postmodern to a fault, prefer Jack Derrida's, "Just the theory, ma'am, just the theory." And when they make a collar, instead of the conventional "Drop it, I got you covered" or "Come on out, we know you're in there," they shout, "All right, time's up. Pens and pencils down."

The Education Police have their own way of Mirandizing a suspect caught reading on an expired library card. They translate their Latin caution—*Licet silentium agere*—into the barbarian tongue for the culturally illiterate mob they deal with daily on the mean streets: "You have the right to remain silent [which goes without saying in a library context]. You have the right to a tutor. If you cannot afford a tutor, one will be appointed for you by the Learning Skills Center."

The uses of Federal Ed Cops go on and on: tracking down students with more than three unexcused absences, running stolen footnotes to ground for the Plagiary Division, and, of course, rounding up warm bodies for committee meetings. Instead of the traditional Missing Persons Bureau, the Ed.D. sports a Division of Anonymous Authors. The members of an elite tactical unit known as the Trivium must complete appropriate terminal degrees before getting their license to kill. They receive advanced training in eraser throwing for crowd control. For their final exam they fire hollow-point chalk at talkers and swoop down on test-takers, bull horns rampant, warning, "Eyes on your own paper."

The halls of ivy—or in my case in the Midwest, the halls of corn and soybeans—will rest easier knowing that Department of Education inspectors will be armed. The British Instructional Police—the subject of a popular BBC dramatic series called "The Invigilators"—only carry weapons when they teach Joyce and Yeats. I understand the French give their school inspectors commissions in the Legion of Deconstruction.

If you know what's good for you, you won't mess around with the Ed Cops. They have red pens and they know how to use them. You say you want to split an infinitive? Go ahead, make my day.

Selling Correctness

One effect of the language police is to make people worry more about their language. And this in turn opens up a market for correctness entrepreneurs. For those who can't be beaten into submission, there's nothing left but the *sales pitch*. If you want my advice, rather than worry about your language, you should worry about ads that encourage you to worry about your language and pay for that privilege at the same time.

Literary magazines have always carried ads catering to the linguistically insecure. Here's an example from a 1928 issue of the *American Mercury*. The text asks, in large print, "Are you embarrassed by mistakes in pronunciation? Nothing reveals your culture—or lack of it—so surely." There's a picture of four people at a formal dinner. We see only the backs of two men's heads. Two women are clearly visible—one is talking, while the other stares at her, perhaps in dismay over her pronunciation.

If you lack confidence in your pronunciation, the ad continues, "you have probably avoided any but the most ordinary words. You are cheating yourself of a tremendously effective social and commercial asset. *And it is no longer necessary.*"

Of course, help is at hand in the form of the *Pronunciphone Method*. For only $11.85, a paltry sum to the likes of those who in 1928, just a year before the Big Crash, sat at formal dinners such as the one pictured, a set of seven records and a booklet called "Good Taste in Speech" will show you how to pronounce two thousand words, including, I hope, how to pronounce *pronunciphone*. The ad asks, with a high-toned subject-verb inversion, "How many of these words *dare* you use in conversation?" There are proper names like *Beethoven, Aphrodite*, and *Buenos Aires*. Other words considered difficult—remember, this was 1928—are *psychiatry* and *Fascism*. Then there are words no well-pronounced person can afford to ignore: *cognoscenti, gauche, naive, incongruous, faux pas*, and, of course, *verbosity*, which is what you'd be guilty of if you used the two thousand words on the records.

Here's a more up-to-date example of an appeal to language suckers culled from the June 1989 issue of a popular writer's magazine sold in most grocery stores. It's for a correspondence course on writing and it is headed *grammar abuse*. That's a tricky phrase; it links language mistakes with such distasteful crimes as child abuse and substance abuse. And though it isn't against the law, at least not yet, grammar abuse is clearly serious stuff.

"Editors agree," goes the text, "it's one of the leading causes of manuscript rejection. And there's the real tragedy: writers with colorful imaginations, creative ideas, and natural writing talent are being held back by poor grammar skills . . . and they don't have to be!" Which, translated into my brand of English, means "Why should writers be expected to know how to write?"

The answer to that question is obvious: they shouldn't. Now, with the *Effective Writing* course these hucksters are peddling, you get a guidebook, an instructor to guide you, a generous supply of manuscript-sized envelopes, in case you write anything in the two years they give you to complete the course, and a discount on other writing guides published by the school. All of this for only $125—what did you expect? Prices have gone up since 1928.

The ad encourages you to "invest in yourself now," which translated into grammatical English means, "We need your money more than you do," and it provides a convenient 800 number for impulse shoppers.

Of course I'm not going to spend my money on a course that commits grammar abuse in the name of curing it. For, according to the ad, manuscripts show grammar abuse when they are "riddled with misused or misspelled words, improper punctuation, or other grammatical errors."

These writing experts evidently think that spelling, punctuation, and usage mistakes are grammatical errors. They are not; they are spelling, punctuation, and usage mistakes. Grammar mistakes are errors in morphology and syntax. At least that's how language experts sort things out. True, the general public confuses grammar with spelling and everything else related to language. There's nothing wrong with that. But if these folks are supposed to be experts on language you'd think they'd use the term correctly—that's what the language suckers are paying them for anyway—and it is clear to me that language experts, they ain't.

If you want an expert, don't throw away your money, take my word for it. Of course if you've spent money on my book, instead of borrowing it from your public library, you may have a problem. Unlike most retailers, bookstores are not big on returns.

The Giant Vocabulary Enhancer

You can't change your pronunciation by listening to records, and you can't increase your word store by buying any of those vocabulary aids you hear advertised on the radio. You know the ones I mean, the ones where an important-sounding voice intones, "People judge you by the words you use." Which of course is true, but that doesn't mean you should run out and buy a set of cassette tapes, or even one of those new-word-a-day calendars, to teach you hard words. Because people won't be impressed with you if you use sesquipedalian lexis. No, they'll be annoyed that you're using words they don't know, like *sesquipedalian*, which means 'foot-and-a-half-long,' and *lexis*, which means vocabulary—or they'll simply consider you pretentious. And you shouldn't have to buy a vocabulary builder to know what *pretentious* means.

Even if you really did want to learn long words, listening to tapes while you're stuck in traffic is not the way to do it. Years ago the language-meisters (not to be confused with real teachers, who run a not-for-profit shop) went on a learn-in-your-sleep binge. It seems that psychologists had proved you could assimilate knowledge while you slept, and this resulted in a flurry of ads for records and tapes that taught everything from French to calculus by means of a little speaker you put under your pillow. The problem was that this new sleep learning did not produce a generation of people whose French or calculus was noticeably improved. And the little speakers weren't all that comfortable to sleep on.

So I predict the same sort of success rate for the cassettes you just flip into your car's tape player and sit back to absorb. In fact what will probably happen is that people will fall asleep at the wheel while listening to the boring words being slowly and meticulously pronounced, defined, and used in even more boring sentences. Perhaps you have occasionally wished this fate on big-word users.

There's only one surefire way to learn words, and it's not memorizing lists or listening to them being read aloud. Read books, magazines, cereal boxes, signs, memos, letters, anything that has words arranged into meaningful sentences and paragraphs. And write. You'll learn efficiently and quickly and you won't make the kind of embarrassing errors, or faux pas, that people who learn their words from tapes and calendars are likely to make.

What Do Usage Guides Tell You, Anyway?

Lower-tech than records and tapes, usage guides provide the basic ammunition for the language police. Right before I got this question about usage guides, a new one crossed my desk, so I thought this would be the perfect opportunity to give those of you who haven't recently dipped into a good usage guide an idea of what you can find there.

The book we're looking at is the *Longman Guide to Good Usage* (usage guides do not have sexy titles). But it might be any similar guide, as its contents are typical of the usage book ilk: it defines literary terms; it tells us the proper plurals of nouns like *tomato* (is there an *e?*); and it gives the correct pronunciation and meaning of common foreign terms like *entree*.

For something a bit more meaty, take the entry for *adapted*, where we find the comment, "This word cannot replace *suited* or *suitable*, because it implies change. Do not write *He's not adapted to violent exercise."* That's all well and good, but you certainly can't say "He's not suitable to violent exercise," and I wonder whether you should even say "He's not suited to violent exercise," as the folks at Longman recommend. For one thing, it's in the passive voice.

If we look under *passive* in the Longman usage guide we are given the standard advice on active and passive voice: "We recommend the active unless there is good reason for using the passive." What constitutes good reason for using the passive is seldom stated, since most of these guides assume there is never a good reason to do so. This advice is followed by a complicated and difficult to follow explanation—a page and a half, with eight subheadings—of why the passive voice is complicated and difficult to follow. Why Longman doesn't follow its own advice and recommend the active "Violent exercise doesn't suit him" is too complicated for me to figure out.

But let's go on to the entry for *Ms*. Assuming no prior knowledge of this word, Longman tells us right up front, "This title shows that the person named is a woman, just as *Mr.* indicates a man." Sometimes usage guides feel the need to confirm the obvious. We are then told that the term conceals marital status, but since the folks at Longman want to make sure we didn't miss this important point, they add: "*Ms.* is used either with or without a woman's first name, though not with her husband's first name." Well, I should think not. The editors then tell us *Ms.* is outlawed by the *New York Times* style manual, a statement which was true some years ago, but was not true by the time the Guide was published.

Don't get me wrong. The *Longman Guide* is occasionally correct. It tells us that the distinction between *shall* and *will* is dying out, as is that between *can* and *may:* both can be used nowadays to indicate permission. It mentions that some people accept *alright* as one word, though it advises against the usage. And it reminds us that the people of the Soviet Union are *Soviets,* not *Russians* (Russia is one of the republics of the USSR, as events subsequent to the publication of the Longman guide have made more clear to English-language readers), just as the term *British* includes not only the English, but the Irish, Scots, Welsh, and immigrants who have become citizens of the United Kingdom, while *American* can refer both broadly to inhabitants of the New World and specifically to United Statesers, who alas have no other convenient adjective (*Usans* and similar invented terms have not had much luck). I assume that with the decline of the former Soviet Union, Longman has already revised its note on *Soviet.*

Longman gives you the proper, neutral way to refer to blacks (not Negroes, though in many cases now in the United States, African Americans), Jews (not Hebrews), Asians (not Asiatics or Orientals), gays (not queers), and Muslims (not Mohammedans). It tells you that *au naturel* means 'cooked plainly,' or 'naked,' reminds you to spell it *-el,* not *-al,* then tells you to "avoid such foreign phrases," as you may use them incorrectly or intimidate your audience. The editors add, "It is of course another matter if unethically one actually wants to make someone feel inferior."

So that's it: usage is not simply being correct, it is being ethical as well. At least that's the underlying message of these usage guides—which dispense a liberal dose of incorrect or at best oversimplified information which, ethically or not, is ultimately designed to play on our fear that our own language use is inferior. Why do they do this? Because, as Willie Sutton said when asked why he robbed banks, that's where the money is.

The Vision of St. Louis

Despite our best, and often our worst, efforts to change other people's language, it seems that language change can't be readily imposed by the language police, the word hucksters, or the usage mongers. It has to come from within. But here's a case of a spontaneous linguistic conversion that's a little too good to be true.

In 1938, the usage critic Charles Allen Lloyd reported a remarkable story about how contemplating the American flag caused a Danish immigrant to lose her accent. It seems that soon after the seventeen-year-old came to the United States with her family, her wealthy father was cheated out of his money and she began to hate both her new country and its language. With time, through the intercession of an unnamed religious group, this hatred softened, she learned English, and her English eventually became excellent. But even after a dozen years she still spoke with an accent which Lloyd says "stamped her at once as a foreigner." One day she had a vision, and everything changed. As Lloyd tells it,

> Seated one evening on a bench in a St. Louis park, she was idly watching the folds of the American flag floating over a government building near by, when there came over her the thought of what that flag stands for—freedom of speech, freedom of religion, freedom of the individual to make his own way and be judged for himself rather than for his ancestors. A great love for America and Americans swept over her—a love so strong as to include even the rascally Americans who had swindled her father. She went home much uplifted, and went about her duties as usual on the following days, but noticed that whenever she spoke, people looked at her strangely. Finally, on the third day, a good friend asked her, "What has become of your Danish accent?" and she realized suddenly that it had been gone since that miraculous moment in the park. [*We Who Speak English* (New York: Crowell, 1938 [rpt., 1939]), pp. 298–99]

Sudden loss of foreign accent in a twenty-nine-year-old woman presents a case for the neurologist, not the grammarian. It is like those stories of people having strokes or getting hit on the head and waking up being able to speak Aramaic or Urdu; and, like the story I call "The Vision of St. Louis," they also turn out to be fake.

In any case, foreignness is frequently an underlying issue in usage guides. The most xenophobic guides promise to rid speakers of English as a second or additional language of their tell-tale errors. As with most such books, however, Lloyd's primary targets are the linguistically insecure native speakers, the "we" of his title who speak English, whose language falls short of our own expectations, and the expectations of those who evaluate us. He concludes that all Americans can improve their own English so that it more closely approximates the ideal of the correct standard, unaccented by error. Yes, we should all use language better (and for most of us, according to Lloyd and usage critics like him, better usage would indeed seem to be some kind of miracle). But calling for linguistic improvement, whether through assiduous practice in a workbook or meditation on a patriotic object, is a piety that is frequently expressed and virtually meaningless.

Lloyd's little story further presumes that accent is nothing but a state of mind, and it suggests, contrary to fact, that speakers of English have no accents or dialects, that they commune cheerfully and freely with one another, much like Milton's angels in *Paradise Lost*. A linguist reading this story will certainly wonder what accent replaced the lost accent of the once-melancholy Dane whose ethnicity was miraculously thrown into the melting pot with all the rest. Was it an American accent of the South Midland variety? To what extent was it modified by the urban environment of St. Louis? By the speaker's age? Her sex? Her social class? Her peers? Her level of education? Her anonymous but reconciling religious affiliation? Her favorite movies or radio programs (remember, this was supposed to have happened in 1938)? If accented speech is regarded as potentially subversive, as it often has been in the United States during economic downturns or periods of war, then how many acknowledged American patriots of foreign birth would Lloyd and his successors have us reclassify?

In reality, English in America, as it is throughout the world, is both rich and various, though that richness and variety is often as suspect as a foreign accent. But even as we celebrate cultural diversity in American society and American literature, we fear and reject diversity in the American language, where correctness and standardization (terms that to my mind remain unconstitutionally vague) remain the academic goals. It's one thing to explode the literary canon and rewrite the syllabus in the name of cultural pluralism, but quite another to allow students to practice linguistic diversity in the classroom.

Like English Only advocates, supporters of standard English have specters to raise. They insist that without enforced standards of correctness, language will decay, communication will break down, and civilization will disappear. Literacy, already imperiled, will deteriorate even further. Although such warnings have been noised about for some centuries now, evidence suggests that language variety is a sign of health, not decay. It is more likely that English will meet its end through the inappropriate splitting of atoms, not infinitives; through global warming, not subject-verb disagreement.

Charles Allen Lloyd's vision is an appropriate one to deconstruct as we quarrel over education in America: Is it only OK to be culturally diverse so long as we do it in the same uniform and unaccented language, so long as we show no trace of being foreign or incorrect, so long as our words carry the imprimatur of the language police?

For Lloyd, American society and language come from many sources. In the melting pot there is strength. Out of the many comes one, as it says in the American monetary motto, *e pluribus unum*. And Standard English, says the vision of St. Louis, is the glue that holds our centrifugal society together, the linguistic "one," like the social, deriving from the "many." But Standard English is not one language indivisible. It is, if anything, a collection of loosely defined and ever-shifting standards continually adapting themselves to the infinite number of contexts where language is used. So pursuit of the one true standard of correct English is doomed to fail.

And, of course, the American motto is in Latin, not English, but that's beside the point. Or is it?

5 Teaching English

Digging through the files in my office I came across a guide to freshman writing at the University of Illinois for 1969. The '60s are a long way away and sometimes we remember them—those of us who are old enough, that is—through a selective filter (I'd say through rose-colored glasses but that's a cliché, and teachers of writing try to discourage freshmen from using clichés). But if we remember the '60s, fondly or not, as a mixture of long hair, protest, and bell-bottoms, then a look at the 1969 guide to freshman writing will confirm those memories as an accurate picture of the times.

And *picture*, it would seem, is the operative word here. Because what happened to writing at the university in 1969 was that it was replaced by pictures. To use the words of the then-director of freshman writing, "There is, we have learned, a 'visual' literacy; 'composition' may now be viewed as putting things together to achieve coherent communication, whether the 'things' are words, or words and music, words and art-work, or multi-media."

The director told students that, since "written expression is not the sole criterion of intelligence," they could satisfy the two-semester freshman writing requirement by watching movies instead of reading, by singing or dancing or drawing or, if that proved too hard—I mean too repressive as well as too difficult—by cutting out pictures from magazines and pasting them on poster board. At the time, that seemed a revolutionary picture to be painting of the writing program, though today it looks to us more like a blueprint for illiteracy. In 1969, the research paper was out, the collage was in. In the New Age of the paste-up, class discussion didn't focus on paragraph coherence, but on rubber cement. And if you wanted extra credit, you didn't write more, you made a super-8 movie. It's a good thing the camcorder hadn't been invented yet, or we would surely have been subjected to "America's Funniest Home Freshman Themes."

The '60s were seen as a second Renaissance, though more enlightened and relevant than the first rebirth a few centuries before. The freshman writing manual advised instructors to use magazines instead of essays because magazine articles are "more relevant." *Relevant* actually became a cliché in 1968 in New York and California, but it didn't reach the Midwest until the following year. From the enlightened perspective of the '90s, the '60s seem old-fashioned,

"Pictures down 3, to 879 words, in a day of active trading."

quaint, naive, and, well, not all that enlightened; in short, they too were a cliché, though we didn't know it at the time.

If prose was oppressive in 1969, the solution proposed was not to make it less oppressive, but to sing or draw instead. And the prose of the freshman writing manual was oppressive. All men were brothers in that pseudo-egalitarian age. But women were excluded. Through the tyranny of the generic masculine, all teachers and students were referred to as *he*. Though many women taught freshman writing and many more were students in the course, they were non-persons; their pronouns never appear. It may have been a revolutionary time, but it was not a liberating one.

Now, I have left out a lot in my own picture of writing instruction at the U of I in 1969. For one thing, while some students were busy tracing sketches from matchbook covers, others were writing papers on John Milton and reading Plato. I have intentionally made the '60s sound medieval, and I did this because the '60s, just like the Renaissance, promoted the idea that they were not just special, but a quantum leap better than what had come before. The middle ages were invented by the Renaissance to make people in the Renaissance feel better about themselves. Like Renaissance men *and women*, people in the '60s felt disdain for the past, the Ozzie and Harriet '50s. They saw themselves as giants standing on the shoulders of dwarfs, to use yet another historical cliché.

From our own exalted perspective we may shudder at the thought of students pasting their way through freshman comp. A colleague of mine, who eventually became responsible for putting the writing back in freshman writing at Illinois, remembers seeing a student walking out of the last composition class of the semester, research poster rolled up under her arm, saying to a friend, "I hope I never see another collage again." Which is exactly what students used to say, and say again today, about their term papers after turning them in.

I was eight years past being a freshman in 1969, and six years would pass before I arrived to teach at the University of Illinois, and I never took freshman composition in college anyway, but I like to think that even if I had been eight years younger, running loose with a Magic Marker, scissors, and paste, instead of a pen, I would still have read books, not comics, and still have preferred writing to layout.

Susie Scribbles

I am a writer and a writing teacher. I've been in the writing dodge all my life. But I do other things as well, and with two small children (and a third full-grown), one of the things I find myself doing frequently is visiting toy stores. Just recently these two previously unconnected halves of my life, writing and toys, finally came together in the form of Susie Scribbles.

Susie Scribbles, marketed by Wonderama for the hefty price of $119.95 (you'd think at that price they'd throw in the four C batteries), is a doll that writes. There she was, sitting in a big red box in the doll aisle of the local *Palais des Enfants*—any toy that expensive can't be sold in plain old Children's Palace.

A picture on the box shows the doll, holding a crayon, writing on a piece of paper. And a legend on the box proclaims, "Whatever I say I write. Just like a real kid."

Now I don't make a lot of money from writing, so I'm not about to pop for the price of admission just to see the amazing Susie Scribbles go through her act. I've been disappointed by dolls before. But this latest addition to the increasing stable of robot toys piques my curiosity. First of all, there's the question of the claim, "Whatever I say I write. Just like a real kid." While this may be true in Susie's tape-and-C-battery-driven robot world, real kids don't write whatever they say. Many of them do say a lot, but most of them don't write much at all, and when they do the result is often different from actual speech, as it should be.

Then there's the implicit claim that writing is so easy even a doll can do it. Before you accuse me of trying to keep writing the exclusive province of human beings, let me say that I am open to suggestion. Machines can learn to play chess. They can solve the five-color map problem. They can even tell me how much is in my checking account, which involves yet more daunting arithmetical calculations. (The software my computer uses to balance my books is called *Quicken*, which means, literally, 'to make alive.') So why not let a machine write? Am I simply afraid I'll become obsolete, that I'll have to be retrained—should I say, reprogrammed—to do something else?

And if the machine that writes is anthropomorphosed into a doll, well, that's just one step closer to replacing real writers, isn't it? Dolls can talk; they've said "Mama" for years. They can even tell stories. Remember Teddy Ruxpin a few holiday seasons ago? That doll prompted a string of story-telling clones, including an echo doll that could repeat whatever you said to it. Talking, it seems, is no longer enough to sell a doll. Now they have to write as well. But, I ask you, what is a doll going to write that anybody would want to read?

All right, I *can* see how Susie Scribbles might revolutionize writing instruction. Take a class of freshman composition students and set them against twenty-two freshly charged writing dolls. After five minutes of warm-up, the dolls are happily clicking away, while the freshmen are still looking around nervously, chewing on their pens, covering their blank paper with their free arms. After fifty minutes, the dolls are still going strong, while the freshmen lie exhausted and bloodied across what is left of their essay booklets. Susie Scribbles could become an instructor's dream. I wonder if a panel of graders could tell the difference between the essays produced by the students and those created by the dolls? I'm sure the dolls would have better handwriting.

Maybe I am just trying to protect my turf. Robots make better cars than people do. So why can't dolls promise to take the human error out of writing? Who am I to stand in the way of progress? Imagine if all that writers needed for inspiration and motivation was a fresh tape and some new batteries. It would be a better world.

But that's not what's going to happen. Human writers won't become more like dolls, dolls will become like human writers. Once these dolls discover that the crayon is mightier than the neutron-blasting laser-sword, they'll hire agents, demand big advances, and appear on talk shows. With success, writing dolls will become temperamental and reclusive. They'll miss deadlines, frustrate editors, and sue unauthorized biographers. They'll consume greater and greater quantities of battery acid and produce less and less prose. Fear of failure and unhappy family lives will drive them into analysis and spark the creation of next season's new doll: the manic-depressive, self-destructive Susie Seconal, who finally ends it all by sticking her head in an Easy Bake oven, and doesn't leave a note.

The Grammar Gene

A recent Associated Press story (Feb. 10, 1992) trumpeted the discovery of a single dominant gene that controls the ability to learn grammar. Indeed. So that's why my grammar lessons always bomb: the students have DNA that is programmed to ignore my instruction.

This grammar gene is serious science, though. A Montreal research team has traced a defect in the grammar gene through three generations of a family suffering from *dysphasia*. According to the researchers, dysphasia is a term applied to a group of symptoms including the late onset of language use in childhood. This is followed by such severe difficulties with pronunciation and sentence formation that sufferers are often not understood until they are seven years old. The condition persists into adulthood, though dysphasics often learn to disguise their communication problem by planning out ahead of time what they are going to say or avoiding, as far as possible, situations in which they must use language publicly (M. Gopnik and M. Crago [1991], "Familial Aggregation of a Developmental Language Disorder," *Cognition* 39: 1–50).

No one has actually found this grammar gene, though postulating its existence is supposed to explain why sixteen members of a Montreal family of thirty, ranging in age from 74 on down, could not produce plural nouns or the past tense forms of regular verbs, but were otherwise completely normal in terms of intelligence and cognitive ability.

I've looked at some of the research behind the newspaper story—while it is very suggestive, it is not quite as dramatic as the journalism would have it, and I expect that the genetic explanation will turn out to be more complex than the newspaper accounts allow for. Some language difficulties are clearly inherited. Others may be unique: there's the fictional example of Mrs. Malaprop, who called alligators *allegories,* and the real-life Rev. William Spooner, who regularly mixed up the initial sounds of words to get "queer old dean" when he meant to say "dear old queen." Both have given their names to science: Malapropisms and Spoonerisms are common forms of language error and form the core of many language jokes.

It's no secret as well that children make funny language mistakes all the time. Once my daughter told me that water was an *average* drink. That sounded reasonable, but when she added that soda and juice were also averages, I asked her what she meant, thinking it might have something to do with the new math. Exasperated at the ignorance of her fond parent, she told me that they were all averages because on menus after the food you could eat they had a list of the averages you could drink. When I gently suggested she meant *beverages,* she got mad (what do grown-ups know, anyway?).

Real-world language abnormalities, which affect more than the odd word here and there, are not at all funny. But let's face it, the announcement of grammar genetics is, like cold fusion, an invitation to satire. It may be tempting to posit a past-tense gene (or perhaps, more generally, a gene that controls word suffixes) and to conclude that if I make a mistake in verb tense I must be some kind of mutant (which my English teachers always suspected anyway), but it's more likely that there is less of a direct link between genes and verbs than the researchers suspect.

A genetic variation affecting the structure or workings of the brain may have a variety of consequences, difficulty with certain kinds of language processing being only one. And it does not seem likely that human beings have developed a gene for marking past tense by adding *-ed* to verbs, since there are a number of human languages that do not mark the past tense with suffixes. The dysphasics in the study have real language problems, but they have no trouble with irregular verbs, only regular ones, and they can tell past from present from future as far as real-world events go.

In any case, the grammar gene is just the first step in genetic engineering: suppose there's a reading gene (it would have to be a mutation since reading is a much more recent development in human history than is language), and another for spelling (good readers don't always make good spellers). In fact, the study of grammar genetics smacks of eugenics: find the gene, tinker with it, and improve the breed. Imagine a whole race of superhumans who don't drop their *g*'s or split infinitives. Through selective breeding and intermarriage, we could eliminate dialects in a generation, have everyone in the world speaking the same language in no time at all.

And not just humans, either. With the convergence of genetic and language engineering, you could take a defective past-tense gene and put it in a rat cell. Before long, scores on standardized tests like the RAT go into a tailspin, there's a rat literacy crisis, rat trainers in labs start teaching to the standardized mazes, rat educational critics complain that mazes are culture-biased, and it's *Penguin Island* and *Animal Farm* all over again.

Imagine what Dr. Science could do with this? Of course Dr. Science only has a Master's degree. Dr. Grammar has a real Ph.D. And he says, "The next time your past tense gives you trouble, get your DNA analyzed. It'll do you a world of good."

Creative Evolution

Somebody with nothing better to do once took a whack at the old saw, "You can't have your cake and eat it, too," claiming that the saying should be reversed—"you can't eat your cake and have it, too." They argued that, logically speaking, you must have your cake before you can eat it. If you eat your cake first, then obviously you cannot have it after you eat it because it is all gone. Forward or backward, people have been trying to defeat the obvious meaning of the proverb—"You can't have it both ways"—since the dawn of time.

And speaking of the dawn of time, I've just come upon a pair of books that tries to have it both ways. Hyperion Publishers has produced two handsomely illustrated children's books that describe the dawn of time. Or rather, the dawns of time, for one book, *The Evolution of the World,* is evolutionary, and the other, *The Creation of the World,* creationist. The books are striking examples of parallel universes. Each of the six stages in the creationist book just happens to match a stage in the evolutionary one. Each begins at the beginning, either with the light-producing big bang of the astrophysicists or the "Let there be light" of the divinely inspired first day.

The illustrations accompanying the books are appropriately biblical or Darwinian—the biblical showing a preference for pastel shades in contrast to the primary colors decorating the scientific model. And each version ends on the sixth day or at the sixth stage, depending on your preference, with the peopling of the planet, either the creation of the first couple by divine intervention and some fiddling with a side order of ribs or the evolution of humans from the Great Apes.

At the end of page six in *Creation* the Creator rests, while on the sixth page of the evolutionary version the secular-minded editors declare a weekend.

Is this the fairness doctrine in action: both sides of an issue being given equal time and equal weight? Or is it a crass capitalist attempt to corner the "dawn of time" market by selling, like an arms dealer, to both sides in the ideological war? On the one hand, this paradoxical set of books claims that the universe originated from an unstable configuration of hydrogen under great pressure, and on the other, contends that there's this divine voice illuminating the darkened void. How can they lose? Is it a breath mint or a candy mint? Aparticle or a wave? A floorwax or a dessert topping? Yes, you're both right. Truth is relative, it took six pages to evolve, and everybody's a winner. The publishers, hedging their transcendental bets, laugh all the way to the bank.

Only wait a minute. In the game of the origins of the universe, most people believe only one theory is right. It's like matter and antimatter or, to be fair, god and the devil. The advocates of the losing theory, whichever one it is, are either damned and godless, or closed-minded, anti-intellectual fanatics.

And what if you just can't make up your mind? What if you really want to explore both sides of the issue? Well, then you've really got a problem. Because there are the two books, sitting side by side on the shelf in the bookstore, but you can't buy both of them, not at the same time. If you want to take home the nonsectarian creationist as well as the freethinking evolutionist version, an alarm goes off in the store, the computer automatically voids the transaction, your credit card is impounded, and a note is made in your permanent file marking you as a national security risk and possible corrupter of youth. You may never work in this town again.

If Hyperion Books ever publishes a series on the end of the world to parallel its ambivalent pair on the beginning, my guess is it will produce a tetralogy, a set of four books designed once again to cover all the bases, at least those bases laid out by Robert Frost and T. S. Eliot: one book to claim the world will end in fire; another to claim it will end in ice; a third will end the world with a bang; the last will end it with a whimper.

The Future of English

Speaking of the end of the world, here's another question I got that set off a whole chain of questions and answers: "The reason that

Latin is the language of science is because of its being dead, so that it would never change."

This is clearly not a question, but a statement. And as a statement it is wrong. But it is interesting, and not simply for its use of the often-discredited redundancy "the reason . . . is because"—there's nothing wrong with being perfectly clear twice in the same sentence. It's interesting because it assumes, as most of my questioners do, that language change is not good, and that when something dies, it ceases to change. An examination of the contents of my refrigerator reveals that death does not preclude decay. The leftovers I so carefully tucked into little plastic bowls and then forgot have not only rotted, they have produced newly recombinant life-forms, albeit ones I hesitate to include in my next sandwich.

So did Latin die, but it left a corpus, not a corpse, mutating into what we now call the Romance (from Roman) languages. As for Latin being the language of science, any physicist knows that the language of science is English. Haven't you heard? Latin is dead.

Will what happened to Latin and the other world languages (Greek, French, possibly a couple of others, including whatever lingo they used in the Garden of Eden or wherever things started out)—will that happen to English? There's no sign of English dying out right now, but that is no cause for hubris. As English continues to spread around the globe, to the point where some experts speak of *Englishes* and not just English, the possibility arises that the fragments may develop much the same way that French, Italian, Portuguese, Spanish, and R(o)(u)(ou)manian (use whatever vowel[s] you want) were formed by speakers who thought they were using Latin all along.

A Universal Language (or Two)

According to the Bible, there was a time when everyone on Earth spoke the same language. Communication in those days was easy; no interpreters were needed. Then some folks built a tower up to heaven, but their deity found this presumptuous, so the Tower of Babel was destroyed, and, as further punishment, everyone was made to speak different languages. Translation has been a growth industry ever since.

Experts guess that there are between three and ten thousand different languages spoken in the world today. But, as if this weren't enough, every now and then someone creates an artificial, international, universal language designed to turn the babble of tongues into one clear, rational, and easy-to-learn lingo that would drive the Berlitzes out of business.

Now, it isn't easy to invent a whole new language, let alone to get everyone else to adopt it. But the language coiners have given us several hundred, including Volapuk, Eurolengo, Ido, Idiom Neutral, Novial, and of course the best-known of all, Esperanto, whose very name signifies hope. Of course, like real languages, these artificial languages have their little rivalries. When English speakers don't understand something they may say, "It's Greek to me." In Esperanto, the equivalent idiom is something like, "It sounds like a bunch of Volapuk."

A curiosity among home-made languages is *Solresol*, which employs the notes of the scale—*do, re, mi*, and so on—as the building blocks of words. In Solresol, *si* is 'yes' and *do* is 'no,' while *doremi* is 'day' and *dorefa* 'week.' You speak Solresol in different keys, just like music, reversing syllables to indicate opposites: *misol* is 'good,' *solmi*, 'evil.' And Solresol can be whistled, played, or sung as well as spoken.

For the less musical who still desire a pre-fab tongue, there is Esperanto. Created about one hundred years ago by a Polish eye doctor, it is still used in international conferences, and there are books, newspapers, and radio broadcasts in the language. An article I once wrote appeared with an abstract in Esperanto added by the editor.

The artificial languages have in common a simplified and regular grammatical structure, and a vocabulary of words whose meaning is supposed to be transparent—all you have to do is see or hear the word and you automatically know what it means. They are also supposed to be neutral, not favoring one or another language in their composition. Esperanto has only sixteen grammar rules, and about 15,000 roots from which its words are built; English has half a million words, and enough grammar rules to make sixteen sound attractive. But while international in intent, Esperanto has a Western bias: it is Latin in structure and vocabulary, and Slavic in pronunciation. It retains masculine and feminine forms of nouns, as well as subject and object cases, unmotivated grammatical complications that English spares us. Esperanto relies heavily on combining prefixes and suffixes to form its words, and the results are sometimes not very transparent. *Malsanulejo*, 'hospital,' is composed from the root *sana*, 'health,' combined with the prefix *mal*, 'bad,' and it means 'bad-health-place.' It is also criticized for having a sexist bias since feminine forms are derived from masculine ones. I couldn't read the Esperanto abstract of my article, let alone recognize that it summarized my own writing.

But the big problem with artificial languages is not the difficulty of arriving at universal meaning. Rather it is the naive assumption of their creators that if we all spoke one language, we could achieve world peace, find universal truth, break down cultural barriers, and reduce printing costs, all at one blow. Experience shows that people speaking a single language have as much trouble getting along with one another as people who speak different tongues.

Of course the idea that we don't need a universal language because English is already universal, with as many as 750 million speakers around the world, may be a bit optimistic. English may be international now, but for how long? Before English, French was the world's language, and before French, Latin. And before Latin? Well, have you forgotten the incident at Babel?

Is English Dying?

In the fifth century a group of Angles crossed from someplace in Europe to a largish island west of Brittany. The Angles decided that everyone should speak Angle-ish, or English, in their new home. Ever since, the prophets of doom, with the help of the occasional Irish bard, the entire French Academy, and many of my callers and correspondents, have been predicting or even actively plotting the death of English.

Is English really dying? For years I've been saying no. It's how I earn my living. But what if I'm wrong about English? Suppose the language *is* dying. Suppose it doesn't have enough breath in it to make it to the next millennium, or worse, suppose that it's already dead. So what happens next? Will the relatives scrabble over who gets what? Has English even left a will? Will there be probate? And here's an even more important question: did it jump, or was it pushed?

English is an international language. It took over that role from French, which got it from Latin which got it from Greek (and let's not forget medieval Arabic, which was also international) and so on back to the language of the Garden of Eden (which somebody once insisted was Swedish). In those early biblical days you could call a language international if it was spoken by only two people and a God (not to mention a snake, who had a forked tongue and was probably bilingual).

Anyway we know that every international language so far has died, so even if English isn't dead yet, but is only in a coma being kept alive by word processors, we have to ask the question, after

English, what? Is some language waiting in the wings to take over? Or is it back to Babel for a while, or at least to the Balkans, with a lot of little languages bumping each other around until another bully emerges to dominate once again? And which will that lucky little language be? Maybe we should set up an office pool on which language will be the next world language.

Don't forget that English was once as obscure and unpopular as its critics claim it is again. There are plenty of not-yet-world-class tongues whose present situation is much like that which the newborn English once enjoyed. See what you think:

1. There's Finnish, which is not related to any other language, except maybe Estonian and, remotely, Hungarian. Finnish is what we call an agglutinative language: it recycles words by piling on syllables at the end. As a result, Finnish has very long words that are unrecognizable to anyone who doesn't speak it. Not many people born outside Finland volunteer to learn Finnish.

2. Then there's Basque, which is even less related to other languages than Finnish. Some scholars think Basque is a language left over from before the Indo-Europeans moved into Europe; others trace it to Africa. The Spanish think Basque is a language for blowing things up in. (The French are glad most Basque speakers live in Spain.) Like Finnish, Basque is agglutinative. It has lots of diphthongs, which are basically two-syllable vowels, and in each Basque village the consonants are pronounced differently. The Basque number system is based on twenty, not ten. So 157 in Basque is 7×20+17. Considering how important computers are in today's society, though, it might be better to have an international language with a hexagesimal number system: that's one based on sixteen.

3. Hawaiian is another possibility for international-language status: it has only thirteen sounds. English has forty-four, Finnish thirty-nine. There's a language in New Guinea with only eleven. Having only thirteen sounds should simplify pronunciation quite a bit, but, in fact, non-Hawaiians have some trouble with the glottal stop in words like *muu muu*, pronounced something like *mu-u mu-u*. Another problem is that languages with a small inventory of sounds, like Hawaiian, have to have very long words in order to get anything said at all.

Like English, Hawaiian is a language that was imported to an island. Hawaiian was then virtually wiped out by colonizers, most of whom spoke English. But along with English it is an official language of the state of Hawaii. So perhaps when English is certified as dead by the lexical authorities, Hawaiian will finally come into its own.

Don't hold your breath trying to guess what language my next answer will be in. I once spent a week in darkest Finland in the middle of February (when it was really dark—the sun coming out only between ten and three) and I only managed to learn three words: *aksi*, *kaksi*, and *taksi*, which mean 'one,' 'two,' and 'taxi.' I spent a month in Hawaii and didn't do much better with the language, though I did like the climate a bit more.

The Language of the Universe

It's not enough that we have to worry about communicating with everyone else on the planet. Now we have to worry about talking to extraterrestrials too. A group at NASA, the National Aeronautics and Space Administration, is trying to figure out how to respond if the Earth is ever contacted by aliens using radios.

And why not? We've been sending radio waves out into space for so long that "Fibber McGee and Molly" and "Our Gal Sunday" have just about made it to the nearest stars. What if some interstellar being has heard these shows and sends us a reply? NASA has to be ready, and the Space Agency is inviting us to help out. So here's my contribution to the national effort.

This isn't the first time our rocket scientists have tried communing with the heavens. Back in the '70s a Pioneer spacecraft soared into space carrying a pictorial plaque designed to tell "scientifically educated inhabitants of some other star system" where it came from. NASA has never let on whether any Wookie or Klingon ever replied to the line drawing of a naked human couple posed suggestively next to a schematic representation of the hydrogen atom.

A reply to the pictograph in space would be quite a feat. An alien life form would first have to be able to "perceive" the plaque with something analogous to our eyes. But even if they could surmount that initial hurdle, perception is not enough. How do you know whether the lines scratched on metal are writing or pictures and not just space junk, scratches left by some interstellar shopping cart that blindsided the Pioneer in the parking lot of some 7×10^{11} convenience space station near Andromeda?

It's the same with the radio waves we've been sending out into the unknown: first you have to "receive" them, then you've got to determine that they represent a message instead of random space noise. Even if you are able to glean that the drawing or the radio signals have some significance, you have to have an awful lot of cultural baggage already stowed aboard to parse the significance of a hand raised in a gesture of peace and welcome, or of a long lost Giants game from the Polo Grounds, back in the days before the designated hitter.

And suppose, just suppose, our intergalactic radio buff picks up the Orson Welles Mercury Theatre broadcast that made thousands of Americans think aliens were invading New Jersey? What kind of response is that going to bring from the Milky Way? What if some meddlesome universal peacekeeping civilization not unlike our own decided to send a task force to liberate us from Welles's practical joke? Do you think they'd send a message first, or just pounce down upon us warp speed ahead, phasers set on stun? All earthlings will look alike to the space invaders, who themselves probably look like Orson Welles on a bad day. Their only choice will be to vaporize us all.

Of course that's not very likely to happen, which is why we've made so many movies about the Earth being invaded by extraterrestrials bent on vaporizing all of us or taking over our bodies. If you had a body like Orson Welles you'd want to do the same thing.

In any case, our radiotelescopes are busily scanning the skies for signs of technologically advanced life. But how are our NASA skylisteners going to interpret any radio waves they might happen upon? Even if they can sift the signals from the universal background of electromagnetic radiation, decoding them into meaningful segments of language is going to take a whole lot more than an infinite number of monkeys working at an infinite number of wordprocessors. And you know as well as I do that even if the force is with us and our NASA skydroppers crack the interstellar code, all they'll wind up with are reruns of "The FBI in Peace and War" bouncing back from the far-reaches of space-time, together with sound bites from politicians on Alpha Centauri whose terms expired light years ago, vapid cosmic talk shows on such subjects as "Planets that eat their own moons," and the occasional live report from the Cygnus 1 Sky-Deck Traffic Copter.

Testing, 1–2–3

It's time, once again, for the audience participation portion of the *Guide to Home Language Repair*. As the cops in the mystery novels say,

"I'm the one asking the questions." Which means you, the reader, get to provide the answers. But, gentle reader, since I don't want to leave you hanging, or put undue pressure on you (I've heard all the usual excuses: You didn't have time to study, you were absent, your computer ate your homework), I'll give you the answers as well.

This test comes from *USA Today*, where a headline screams, "Parents: Find out how sharp your language skills are." All you have to do is take the National Homework Test offered by the nation's generic newspaper, fondly known to journalists as "McPaper."

The National Homework Test, which offers questions suitable for students at several grade levels, is supposed to test reading, language, and verbal skills. Now, a newspaper is only going to run such a test if it expects the results to be disastrous: if you miss most of the questions then you fall into the category of "person bites dog," and that makes news. If you score well on these tests, you don't read *USA Today*. You read the *New York Times* and the *Wall Street Journal*.

Anyway, here are some of the test questions. Naturally, they are multiple choice. McPaper can't deal with complex responses. For grade four we have

1. Your memory is your ability to
   a) decide
   b) teach
   c) forget
   d) recall.

The answer may be clear to all of you, but my memory is like a steel sieve, and I am frequently forced to define it in terms of what I forget, not what I remember. My memory is so bad that my nine-year-old daughter has concluded I have what she calls "oldtimer's disease." Furthermore, it's not clear to me how anyone can teach or make decisions without memory: in other words, you could make a case for any of the four answers. Only thirty percent of fourth graders could remember the right answer, which fudgy tests like this one call "the most nearly correct answer" in order to silence critics like me.

Can it be that most fourth-graders remember that *recall* means bringing the family car back to the dealer to fix a defect? What does this say about the sophistication of fourth-graders, or about American technology?

Fourth-graders are also tested on their ability to alphabetize words. This is an essential skill if you do a lot of filing. Less than forty percent of fourth-graders can alphabetize correctly. Not many of them have to file much, either. I'm not so good at alphabetizing myself, and I doubt I was much better in fourth grade—in fact, I'm not even sure alphabetizing was ever part of the curriculum when I went to school. Is this really something that signals a decline in the nation's intellectual strength or does it simply reinforce the notion that school trains people for menial tasks?

But let's move on to some more sophisticated subject matter. What are eighth-graders expected to remember? Here's one teaser:

    2. Where would you probably see this sign—"Horsepower without horse sense is fatal"?

       a) on a highway
       b) on a gym floor
       c) at the track
       d) in a grocery store?

A) is the right answer, according to the testers. Only forty-five percent of eighth-graders can answer this question correctly, but I think the question is flawed. Eighth-graders don't do a lot of driving, unless they've been left back a few times. I've been driving for thirty years and I've never seen a sign like that on a highway. It's a cute warning to speeders, I suppose, but it would take too long to read, especially if you were speeding. Highway signs are short and sweet, like "Buckle Up" or "Speed Radar Timed" or "Exit."

Now comes the real test, the one for eleventh-graders. You have to wade through verbal analogies. Here's one that only twenty-one percent of high school juniors got right:

    3. *Thwart* is to *plan* as

       a) *lose* is to *election*
       b) *fence* is to *field*
       c) *change* is to *pattern*
       d) *slam* is to *door*
       e) *dam* is to *stream*.

The answer is "*dam* is to *stream*," though a strong case could be made for "*change* is to *pattern*" and even "*fence* is to *field*." But we have to accept the answer the test makers chose, even if their logic is fallible.

What do the results of standardized tests tell us? They tell us only how well people take standardized tests, which in turn tells us only whether or not the test takers think like the test makers. The results don't tell us whether this is a good way to think, or why we should all think alike. It is divergent thinking, not consensus, that makes for change, and for what we like to call progress. And divergent thinkers, when they are forced to take tests like this, don't do well on them. They're too busy thinking up alternatives to the right answer, or making up more interesting questions.

To improve the results on things like the National Homework Test, schoolteachers waste a lot of time teaching their students test-taking skills rather than more important things like reading, writing, arithmetic, and complex problem solving. Life, after all, is not multiple choice.

4. Do you
  a) strongly agree
  b) agree
  c) not know
  d) disagree
  e) not care
  f) none of the above?

6 The Copy Shop

In the fall, when schoolbells ring and children sing, the writing teacher's fancy quickly turns to thoughts of plagiarism: the act, though some would call it an art, of passing off another writer's work as your own. In the original Latin, a plagiarist was first a kidnapper or seducer, a committer of crimes whose seriousness underscores the later meaning of the word: a 'literary thief' (*OED*, s.v. *plagiary*).

Imitation may be the sincerest form of flattery, but if you take someone else's words and peddle them as your own, you could find yourself dragged into court and forced to pay handsomely for your crime. To an instructor, plagiarism is a worse evil than low pay, and I have known many a teacher to spend days in the library hoping to find a telltale source in order to punish a student suspected of this capital crime. But according to Thomas Mallon, author of *Stolen Words* (New York: Ticknor & Fields, 1989), while the academic and the literary worlds are scandalized by student plagiarism, they tend to hush up actual instances of the crime by scholars and creative writers, hoping that the specter of such felonious professional behavior will just go away. Mallon, who recounts silent borrowings by such celebrated writers as Laurence Sterne, author of *Tristram Shandy*, and that old albatross Samuel Taylor Coleridge, who silently translated many of his ideas from the work of German philosophers, sees plagiarism as an offense inevitably repeated and seldom skillfully concealed—as if, Mallon says, the perpetrator were crying out, "Stop me before I write again."

According to Mallon, the novelist John Gardner plagiarized a book about Chaucer. When this came to light, Gardner's publishers insisted there had been a minor oversight. They reissued the book with fifty or sixty footnotes on every page. In fact, stolen words don't even attract real attention if big bucks are involved. Mallon tells us that the late Alex Haley reportedly lifted a chunk of his money-making *Roots* from a novel by another writer. Haley's publishers paid an undisclosed but probably hefty settlement (estimated in the hundreds of thousands of dollars) to end the discussion. And remarkably enough, the discussion ended. And when Haley announced he would give his manuscripts and other papers to the University of Tennessee, no one quipped, "Sure, his and who else's?"

Mallon claims that because plagiarism is a crime of one writer against another, its punishment must be a mark, like Cain's: "The sanction most feasible and most just is the ironic one: publication. Get the word out on the persistent offender." Exposure does work. A candidate for a university presidency had to withdraw when a faculty member recognized that the speech he had given as part of the interview process was stolen. Yet, once exposed, the plagiarist often rebounds unscathed. The exposed candidate for president remains a university professor. Mallon tells the story of a Texas Tech history professor who plagiarized his dissertation, several articles, and a book, was discovered during his tenure review, confronted, and quietly allowed to resign. He wound up in Washington working for the National Endowment for the Humanities, judging the written scholarship of others, presumably gathering material for his next book.

Mallon reports that a young American novelist, the son of two members of New York's literary elite, cribbed his much-acclaimed first novel from the first novel of a young British writer, who also happened to be the son of a major British novelist, changing the names and the settings to ones more familiar to American audiences. After a public outcry and apology, the offender slinked off to Hollywood to become the chief writer for a hot show about L.A. lawyers. Of course that's to be expected. It was Dorothy Parker who once said that the only -ism in Hollywood was plagiarism. At least that's what Mallon says she said. I'll take his word for it.

Take My Word for It

Here are some suggestions, which I developed all by myself, on how to deal with plagiarists. Despite our best efforts to root out this worst of all academic crimes, the misappropriation of words has become a way of life in America. Politicians steal words all the time. In fact we expect our public figures to employ a stable of writers to put words into their mouths. Which is why the outcry when Senator Joe Biden borrowed the speech of British politician Neil Kinnock during the 1988 presidential primary season seemed unusual—after all, as Thomas Mallon reports, Jack Kennedy took his famous "Ask not what your country can do for you" line, without acknowledgment, from Oliver Wendell Holmes, or at least his speechwriters did, and Warren G. Harding used it as well. Biden's plagiary may have derailed his presidential campaign, but he remains an influential senator.

Ironically, plagiarism even occurs among plagiarism hunters. A couple of years ago, officials at one Western university admitted lifting the plagiarism section of their freshman writing handbook entirely from materials written at another university in a neighboring state. The offending university simply said it was sorry, and that was the last word on that. But how does such an egregious act of literary piracy play with the students, who are routinely punished for their plagiary with failure and suspension? Perhaps the offending university should be slapped with punishments more like the penalties imposed for athletic recruiting violations: bar the English faculty from conference participation for two years; take away twenty academic scholarships; ban faculty quotes in the *New York Times* and "The MacNeill-Lehrer News Hour." Then maybe people would sit up and take notice. Of course none of this will happen, because writing in America, even in the rare instances when it produces income, is less important than football and basketball, or even field hockey, for that matter.

So what do you do if somebody appropriates your words as their own? Crying "Stop, thief" won't rouse your neighbors—when it's a question of words, people just don't want to get involved. They'll stand idly by while all your worldly thoughts are being hauled away by wordjackers. You could file a stolen words report and let the police take it from there. But the police are not in a position to do much, with so many unsolved cases of word theft still on the books. By now, the investigating officer tells you, shaking her head, your great American novel is in a chop shop in New Jersey, and paragraphs are being faxed to machines all over the country. Nobody's words are safe anymore. Ain't it the truth? Oh, and don't bother to file an insurance claim: in most cases your loss won't exceed your deductible.

You could take the law into your own hands, of course, like some literary Bernhard Goetz, shooting readers on the subway before they have a chance to purloin your letter, slashing books on store shelves in case they have quoted you without attribution. Or maybe you should just count your blessings. Be glad you wrote something worth stealing. After all, you've still got your health and your computer—you can write again. Think about those poor unfortunates with writer's block who can't even rub two words together that anyone else wants to read, let alone make off with.

But don't think I condone plagiarism. On the contrary, I'm agin it; I just don't know how to stop it. Abbie Hoffman once published a book called *Steal This Book.* But he didn't mean it, as anyone who tried to take the title literally would have found out. Go ahead, take my words, I dare you. Violators will be prosecuted to the fullest extent of the law. I'll see you in court.

The Double Standard

Apparently Mallon is right when he claims there is a double standard when it comes to plagiarism. Each day that passes seems to bring news of fresh copying. With the transmutation of East Germany into eastern Germany, Bertolt Brecht has lost his status as culture hero of the (former) GDR and word is freely circulating that Brecht's view of authorship was of the ghostly sort: he subbed out sections of *The Threepenny Opera* and other works "to his mistresses, sometimes for a small percentage of the royalties" (William Madison, "In the Jungle of Archives," *Lingua Franca* [Dec. 1991, 8]). And now comes news of another famous person plagiarizing. The whisperings have become murmurs, the murmurs rumbles. The rumbles in this case, however, show no signs of becoming roars, so untouchable is the person in question. It appears that Martin Luther King, Jr., the great black, now African American, Nobel laureate, and doctor of philosophy (in theology) from Boston University, plagiarized his dissertation. At least so reports Clayborne Carson, writing in the *Chronicle of Higher Education* (Jan. 16, 1991, A52). Carson is the director of the Martin Luther King, Jr., Papers Project at Stanford University, and in that capacity he took great care to confirm what had apparently long been noised about, that King took substantial portions of his doctoral thesis from one done three years earlier by another graduate student sharing the same faculty advisor. It is further suggested that stealing words was a way of life for King, whose graduate and undergraduate papers, together with his oft-reprinted essay, "Letter from a Birmingham Jail," yield further examples of alleged failure to footnote.

The facts concerning the dissertation are not in dispute. To no one's surprise, the interpretation of the facts is a matter of some debate. Unfortunately, all three principals in the affair are now dead, so King cannot explain himself, the "plagiaree" cannot react in dismay or in court to the news, and we cannot ask the dissertation director why he didn't notice King's theft, or why he permitted it (it's not clear which of the latter would be the graver failure). Those who condemn what King did run the risk of being labeled prejudiced iconoclasts. Those who explain it away will be criticized for mindless romanticism and hero-worship. Dealing with plagiarism becomes a no-win situation, though King would certainly have coined, or borrowed, a better phrase to describe the dilemma.

Evidence of King's doctoral plagiarism first came to light three years ago, but an official announcement was made only recently, prompting charges that the news had been suppressed. Though it is clear that most allegations of plagiarism in the academic world take far less time to process (instructor notices something is not right with student essay, makes a trip to the library to locate the source, confronts student), the editors of the King papers insist they could not release the information until they had verified it by laboriously tracking down every reference and checking every detail, displaying a scrupulous attention to research, writing, and editing that their subject, and many other student writers, even at the graduate level, clearly did not share.

How do we react to this news of King's academic irregularity? While some critics have called on Boston University to revoke King's earned doctorate, or to replace it with an honorary one recognizing the work he did rather than the work he stole, others dismiss such suggestions as racist. As one of my more politically astute colleagues put it, nothing happens to middle-class establishment whites who steal the words of others (a statement which Thomas Mallon's book on plagiarism confirms), so why pick on King? The situation is not helped by the resignation of H. Joachim Maitre, dean of Boston University's College of Communication. Maitre's highly personal view of communication permitted him to steal the words of a PBS film critic for a graduation talk he gave. (And, fulfilling the promise that it never rains but it pours, the *New York Times* article reporting the latest B. U. plagiarism lifted, without attribution, some five paragraphs on the story which originally appeared in *The Boston Globe*. According to *Lingua Franca* ("Double Take," [August, 1991, p. 4]),—note how careful I am to give my sources in treading the sensitive minefield of plagiarism—the *Times* admitted that its story was "improperly dependent on the Globe account."

The editors of the King papers, reacting in the soft-pedaling tradition Mallon has outlined, flatly decline to judge King's plagiarism. Says Carson, "Our primary concern was not to determine whether King violated academic rules; it was to assemble evidence regarding the provenance of King's papers." And there was plenty of evidence. According to Carson, stealing a dissertation posed no dilemma for King, who was a habitual recycler of other people's words. In editing the King papers, scholars noticed that he plagiarized many of the term papers he wrote as a student as well, failing to acknowledge or adequately document his sources. (The plagiarism is confirmed and discussed in a special issue of the *Journal of American History*, vol. 78, June 1991.)

But Carson does offer an explanation of King's method of *textual appropriation*, a term he prefers as more general and less invidious than *plagiarism*. According to Carson, while much of the student writing was derivative, King "sought a theological vocabulary that would reinforce [his] core beliefs and enable him to express them with greater precision." Indeed, Carson further sanitizes King's plagiary by explaining that, as a minister "early in his life King learned to express his ideas effectively using the words of others." In other words, plagiarism, the ultimate academic sin, is simply a way of life for the clergy, who have found a loophole in the commandment prohibiting theft. And it is the ministry, not the professors, who are, after all, the guardians of our public morality.

In fact, Carson puts himself in the uncomfortable position of arguing that plagiarism is what helped make King so great: "Our appreciation of King as the pre-eminent American orator of the 20th century is not diminished by recognizing that textual appropriation was one aspect of a successful composition method." While Carson promises that future volumes of the King papers "will continue to present, if necessary, references to the sources of King's words and ideas," this explicit reduction of plagiarism to a "successful composition method" is, at best, a weak defense of an admittedly influential man whose public and private moralities clashed on more than one occasion, and whose papers will be the object of study, even reverence, from the moment they are published.

What is interesting in the King case is not the plagiarism, but the reaction to it. If Thomas Mallon's study of plagiarism is any guide, the King plagiary will cause a stir in the press and then be quickly shunted aside, as if stealing words were no more harmful to society than driving five miles above the speed limit. Keith Miller notes that King not only used unattributed borrowings in his academic work, he used them in his speeches and published writings as well ("Redefining Plagiarism: Martin Luther King's Use of an Oral Tradition," *Chronicle of Higher Education* [Jan. 20, 1993, A60]). Miller prefers to view what King did in the context of a long tradition of ministerial sharing: ideas for sermons, parts of sermons, entire sermons quickly become common property. Other people's words are freely passed around the circuit just as in the wider culture jokes and other stories are freely told and retold.

While it may be easy to accuse Carson of rationalizing King's rhetorical practice, of glossing over a textual crime, we must remember that textual appropriation is indeed a long-approved mode for writers as well as speakers. In "Intertextuality and the Discourse Community" (*Rhetoric Review* 5 [1986]: 34–47), James Porter summarizes the various studies which reveal the sources of Thomas Jefferson's "Declaration of Independence." Jefferson, it seems, silently borrowed most of his most famous phrases, including "all men are created equal" and "Life, Liberty, and the pursuit of Happiness," without attribution, while his attempts at original wording—for example, a denunciation of slavery—were routinely expunged from the final document by his congressional editors, who found them too controversial. Porter concludes, "If Jefferson submitted the Declaration for a college writing class as his own writing, he might well be charged with plagiarism" (37).

I do not propose that we need to rethink the greatness of King or Jefferson or even Coleridge—theirs is a Teflon greatness that mere plagiarism cannot tarnish. What I do find troubling is the clear double standard we commonly apply in judging students against more professional writers. We cajole our charges to do their own work and forbid them to buy their papers from the dark, satanic term-paper mills or to dredge them up from the cross-referenced files of fraternal and sororal organizations. All the while, they write within a literate tradition of intertextuality, where texts copy, silently or with acknowledgment, from one another. And they are surrounded by public figures who pay others to write for them because they can't be bothered to do it for themselves. (I'm not referring only to politicians here: how many best-selling books are of the as-told-to variety?) This situation is nothing new: the *OED* cites an 1863 comment from *Blackwood's Magazine*: "Little wits that plagiarise are but pickpockets: great wits that plagiarise are conquerors." Furthermore, many of these students whom we have cajoled not to copy will enter careers where collaborative, and not individual, writing is the norm, and where they will routinely get the credit or blame for the written work that others do.

Although more than one thoughtful commentator has responded to the King plagiarism by calling for a revaluation of our stance on the issues of originality, shared cultural literacy, and literary property, you can be sure that the academy is not likely to modify its position. Students caught by teachers with plagiary-detecting radar will continue to be punished to the fullest extent, if not of the law, then of the Code on Campus Affairs and the *Handbook of Policies and Regulations Applying to All Students*.

The Devil Made Me Do It

Until recently, one of the most daring attempts I ever heard to beat a plagiarism rap was the photographic-memory gambit. In this bit of bravado, the accused student told a university investigating panel that due to his capacity for total recall, he had unwittingly downloaded his source, word-for-word, from the lofty recesses of his cerebrum. But, alas, the unwitting photographic memorizer failed to call up this ability when an examiner on the panel proffered a book and said, "Well then, just read a couple of pages and repeat them to us."

Comes now, as they say in the archaic language of the law, an even better one, proof that the mind does indeed play tricks on us. A graduate student, expelled from the university for plagiarism, claims that he has a multiple personality disorder and that "one of his personalities submitted the plagiarized paper" without his knowledge. The former student has retained a lawyer and is suing in federal court to get the university to reinstate him.

Now the *in rei* and *corpora delicti* are way beyond me, but I cannot resist telling you that, whatever the disposition of the case, the student's argument as reported in the newspaper (Champaign–Urbana *News-Gazette*, April 3, 1991, 2) is a shoo-in to get the Academy Award for best student excuse concerning a full-length nonoriginal work.

Having one of your personalities submit a stolen paper under your name just to get you in trouble with the teacher is one for the (you should pardon the expression) books. Assuming for the moment that the multiple-personality defense holds up, it presents some interesting problems. Like which personality was the one actually admitted to the university in the first place, and did the university subsequently expel the wrong student? And what about the other personalities? Are they receiving credit for work they didn't do? Are they paying their tuition? What about library fines? "Gee," I can hear him saying, "I never took that book out, but it looks like something my third personality would be interested in." Which one of them takes the tests? Which one fills out the affirmative-action forms?

But aside from the psychoanalytic aspects of the case, there's another matter. There are two traditional ways of looking at authorship: in one, which we may call romantic, we find that no matter what the external influences on a writer, all writing is the product of the individual imagination. According to the opposite view, which for convenience we might call classical (the terms are inexact in their application here), the written text is not the property of the writer but is placed in the writer's mind by a muse who uses the author as a mere vehicle for transmitting ideas. For example, the Homer of the *Iliad* says, "Sing in me, Muse, of the wrath of Achilles," while Virgil begins his *Aeneid* with "Of arms and the man *I* sing." It's a question of who's responsible, of who to credit and who to blame. Or is it *whom?*

So if we were more kindly disposed to plagiarism we might view the multiple-personality defense as a return to a more classical view of authorship, one which submerges the individual and concentrates only on the text. As a matter of fact, throughout much of literary history writers have tried to persuade readers of the truth of their text with claims like "I didn't make this stuff up. I copied it from someone else. Since it's not really my own work, it must be true. And if it's wrong, well that's not my fault." Of course, they were lying: good writers are not mere transmitters but creators. I know this is true because I read it somewhere. Honest, I didn't make it up.

As for "The Case of the Three Papers of Eve," my guess is that the courts won't want to touch it. Or them.

When Professionals Plagiarize

This is my last word on plagiarism. Or somebody's last word, anyway. Days after Mr. Multiple Personality's suit was thrown out of court, the university was rocked by yet another plagiarism story. This time it wasn't a student but a colleague, the director of the highly competitive University High School, a selective-admissions school whose graduates have included Nobel laureates and Pulitzer winners.

The Uni High director, who is supposed to be a model influence on his charges, admitted plagiarizing a federal grant application. He was caught by one of the government's peer reviewers, who recognized the material and blew the whistle (details of the actual plagiarism and its source have not been released, so I can't tell you any more). The plagiarist acknowledged his cheating and resigned both from the directorship of the high school and from his lucrative position—for an academic—as a tenured professor in the College of Education. But he left with a year's salary and, I imagine, his retirement benefits intact, a buy out that cost the university, and the taxpayers of the state, a lot less than dragging the whole affair out in court.

His excuse for breaching the trust placed in him by students, parents, and colleagues? Too much pressure, too little time. As if a difficult task were a license to cheat. Of course everyone publicly expresses sorrow at a fruitful career now off the rails for good. No one publicly says, "How dare he?" or "I always wondered whether he ever had an original idea in his life," which are my outraged reactions. Partly we are all too polite and embarrassed (remember what Mallon said in this regard); partly we may wonder as well whether we too are guilty.

I'll come back to that last point in a moment. Here's a parallel story. The same week the Uni story broke, an instructor referred a plagiarizing student to me (it was that time of year, and one of my administrative functions is to advise instructors on how to deal with plagiarists). The student had a writing assignment due and instead of doing his own work he co-opted the work of a friend of his roommate's, who had handed in a similar assignment for another instructor the year before (it is not clear to me whether cash changed hands during the transaction; I did not inquire). The plagiarist was caught because he neglected to edit the borrowed paper to conform to the demands of the new assignment. All he really would have had to do was change a few key names and he might have gotten away with it. Oh yes, he also forgot to make sure the type face of the paper matched the type face of the new title page he managed to work up, but as he told me, he had pulled an all-nighter (not, presumably, to work on this paper) and he was a bit tired. His punishment, imposed by the instructor, and approved by me, was failure in the course. His excuse for handing in someone else's work as his own? Too much pressure, too little time.

What are we to make of all this? Is the copy virus reproducing itself more virulently? Is academic pressure really a factor? Should caught plagiarists consider taking holy orders? Or do plagiarists simply have a low moral threshold?

Mallon suggests that plagiarism, like shoplifting, is a compulsion rather than a one-time event. Like forgers, plagiarists will make a life of crime, given the chance. In defense of plagiarism you might argue that ideas, once uttered, should belong to everyone. But you certainly can't argue for the universality of intellectual property if plagiarists use other people's writing for personal gain.

Right now I'm more concerned with the personal than with the legal or moral or economic response to plagiarism. Since I seem to be surrounded by a sea of copying, I find myself questioning my own writing: how can I know for sure that my ideas are really mine, that I haven't stored away what others have said, only to trot the words out later, undigested but stripped of their source? We each have, after all, a background of ideas whose provenance is uncertain or ill-remembered. How easy it would be to accidentally blend my own idea with someone else's. Even if I rely on notes I took in the past, how can I be absolutely sure I remembered to differentiate summaries from direct quotes from my own comments and reactions to another writer's text in the cramped space of a three-by-five index card?

I'm sure all writers do that from time to time (when they are successful writers we say they have been "influenced" by other writers; otherwise they're just literary hacks). And there's also the fact that people do come up with the same ideas, sometimes even the same wording, independently. But plagiarists don't make independent discoveries or blend other people's ideas with their own from time to time; they use other people's ideas instead of their own. And they don't just do it on one page, they do it everywhere they write. Only, as Tom Lehrer once wrote, they call it research.

While some plagiarists may take the trouble to rearrange the prose and change the names, most think that's really too much like work. Those who actually patch together a cribbed paper so skillfully that the seams don't show realize in retrospect that their task was harder than researching and writing an original one. But plagiarists are anything but practical, and many lay claim to a boughten or stolen document simply by putting their name in front of it.

And there's another problem in all this plagiarism mess as well: the disparate punishment allotted to students and professionals who cheat. Students, who are really only cheating themselves, whose plagiarism might come under the heading of victimless crime, usually feel the full force of academic law—failure, expulsion, a blemished record that will haunt them for life. But, as Thomas Mallon so carefully documents and as the cases discussed here confirm, professionals who cheat, whether they are writers, professors, or public figures, get off easy, a slap on the wrist, a year's pay, a contract for a new book, probably a strong letter of reference as well so they can land on their feet, ready to strike again.

Unlike our software and our videotapes, our words cannot be copy-protected. And there's some who would allow that's a small price to pay for the freedom to write.

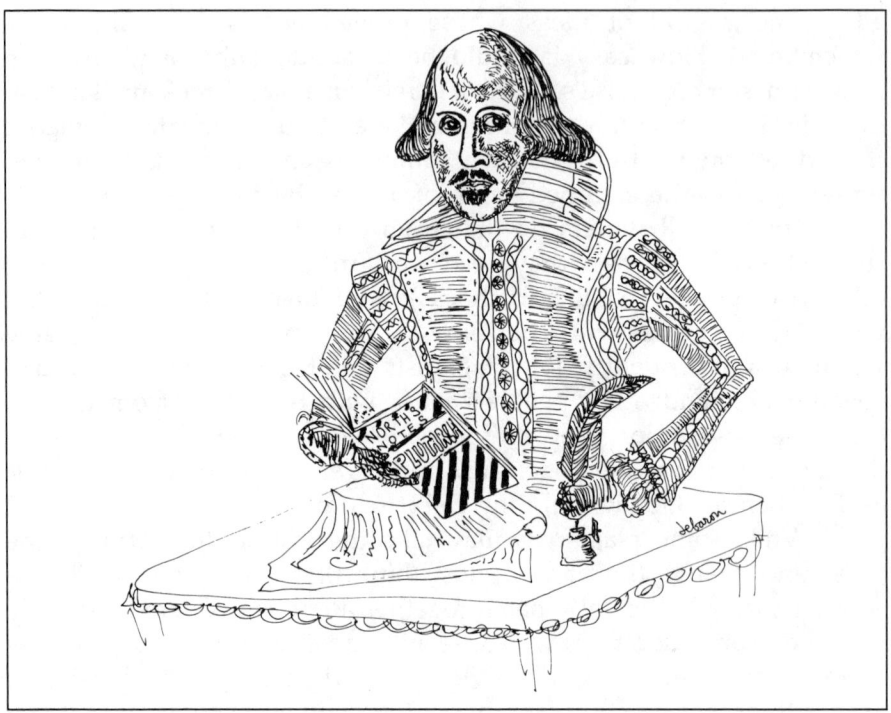

The Shakespeare Test

Following all this heavy discussion of the uncertainties of authorship, it's time for another test. Appropriately enough, it's a test on Shakespeare. Shakespeare is an author who depended heavily on sources without always citing them. He's also a writer whose own authorship has occasionally come under attack by quacks reluctant to believe he could have written as well as he did.

First, though, a few words on testing. By now you've noticed that there are tests to determine if you know enough to get into school, tests to exempt you from various school requirements, tests to measure whether you learned anything in school, tests to permit you to graduate from school, and tests that tell you, once you have graduated, whether or not you will be allowed to pursue the profession for which you took all those tests in the first place.

The question is, is all this testing worth it? Do standardized tests measure anything more than just how good people are at taking standardized tests? This emphasis on testing is something fairly new. Shakespeare didn't take the SAT or the LSAT or the MCAT to be

The Copy Shop

allowed to write plays. It's not even clear that the greatest English playwright even went to school. But suppose that Shakespeare had to take a standardized test? What would a sixteenth-century version of the ACT—the Avon Calling Test—look like? Here are some sample questions:

1. The *Bard of Avon* best describes
   a) a neighborhood tavern.
   b) a line of cheap English cosmetics.
   c) a large white bird that hangs around sailor's necks.
   d) the Earl of Oxford.

2. Complete this quotation with the most nearly correct phrase: *The quality of mercy is not strained; it falleth like the gentle rain from heaven*
   a) upon the fruited plain.
   b) upon my word.
   c) up on the boardwalk.
   d) on the sunny side of the street.

3. Which is the most correct version of Marc Antony's words on the death of Julius Caesar?
   a) This was the unkindest cut of all.
   b) This was the most unkind cut of all.
   c) This was the most unkindest cut of all.
   d) Keep up your bright swords, for the dew will rust them.

4. What word or phrase is the best synonym for *'zounds?*
   a) yipe
   b) geez
   c) oy veh
   d) curses, foiled again.

5. Complete the following analogy: Othello, the Moor of Venice, is to the beast with two backs, as
   a) the gondola is to the gondolier.
   b) the straw is to the camel.
   c) Hamlet is to Rosencrantz and Guildenstern.
   d) Gargamel is to the Smurfs.

6. Which of the following statements is most true?
   a) Cowards die many times before their deaths.
   b) There's a divinity that shapes our ends.
   c) I am but mad north-north-west.
   d) It is the stuff that dreams are made on.

7. Place the following statements in the best order:
   a) She should have died hereafter.
   b) Out, out brief candle.
   c) All our yesterdays have lighted fools the way to dusty death.
   d) It is a tale told by an idiot.

8. Which pairs form the best opposites?
   a) Methought it lifted up its head. / A thousand crowns, or else lay down your head.
   b) I thank your lordship, it is very hot. / It is indifferent cold, my lord, indeed.
   c) Let the white death sit on my cheek for ever. / O bosom black as death.
   d) Come, come, you answer with an idle tongue. / Go, go, you question with a wicked tongue.

OK, ready for the answers? They are A, D, C, B, C, C, ABCD, and D. If you got all eight right then you are probably the author of Shakespeare's plays. If you scored between five and seven, then you are the Earl of Oxford. Less than five, you're barred from playing racquetball for a Division I school. If you got less than two right, you must sign up for Ye Olde Stanleigh Kaplaine's cram course in language repair.

Don't worry if you didn't do well, though. Shakespeare himself failed the test because he didn't have a sharp number two quill.

7 Politically Correct Language

One morning as my daughter was on her way to school, she passed a four-year-old boy who lives down the block. Like most of the four-year-old boys our kids hang out with, Eli was heavily into guns and swords and anything that could be made to function as or even faintly resemble a gun or sword. Seeing Rachel, who was all of nine at the time, he approached in mock assault, weapons at the ready, yelling in the most threatening basso a four-year-old can summon up, "You're a dead man, lady."

This, of course, brings us to the question of gender-neutrality in language.

Sister Suffragette

A radio talk show host called me to ask me to settle a question about the difference between *suffragettes* and *suffragists* which had been plaguing him for a week. It seems he'd made the mistake of referring to *suffragettes* on the air, and he was besieged by listeners, as well as by his own producer, who insisted the proper term is *suffragist*. So after he'd put his foot in it, I was supposed to lead him out of what he calls "the quagmire of the English language."

I guess his problem derives not from the honest mistake he made, if indeed it is a mistake, but from the fact that he views English as a quagmire, both a mess into which he has stepped, and a trap from which someone else must extricate him.

So first, let's look at the words. *Suffragist* is the older term, going back to the 1820s, and it is the more general term as well, referring to the struggle to give the vote to any of several groups who had been denied it. During the American Civil War period, suffragists supported voting rights for African Americans. Later in the century, the term became identified with the struggle for women's voting rights, and it continues to serve as the term of choice to describe the international "Votes for Women" struggle.

Suffragette was coined in 1906 by a journalist writing in London's *Daily Mail* to describe in a derisive manner the newly militant British suffragists: members of the Women's Social and Political Union, led by Emmeline Pankhurst and her daughter, Christabel. Spurred by a refusal of British political leaders to take action on the woman's vote, members of the WSPU switched from education to direct action, demonstrating, interrupting political speeches, breaking windows, even pouring acid on the golf greens where government leaders liked to spend their weekends. When they were imprisoned, these militant suffragists began hunger strikes and endured painful forced feeding. On the linguistic level, they embraced the negative label *Suffragette* and turned it into a badge of honor. Christabel Pankhurst edited a journal called *The Suffragette,* and the Suffragettes (with a capital S) are credited with forcing the British government to acknowledge the rightness of their cause.

While *suffragist,* not *suffragette,* was the term most widely employed earlier in this century by supporters of women's voting rights in the United States, *suffragette* (with a small "s") eventually became the common term in American as well as British English to refer to any member of that early movement, or more generally, any female advocate of women's rights. Since the 1970s, however, a greater sensitivity to the negative connotations of words ending in *-ette* and *-ess* has brought the more neutral *suffragist* back into favor. By the way, lots of Americans today know of the Suffragettes from the song "Sister Suffragette" in the Walt Disney movie, *Mary Poppins,* though there is no reference to the movement in the novel by Pamela L. Travers from which the film was derived.

So much for the vocabulary lesson. What about this pervasive notion that English is a great bog waiting to trap the unsuspecting speaker in inextricable error? Does the path to correctness wind unpredictably through minefields set by some vindictive evil spirit who laughs in hideous anticipation each time we journey forth?

Of course not. But it does seem that way to a lot of folks who think of English teachers as munitions experts. And to radio commentators, because every time we open our mouths, the mad bomber gleefully writes in to tell us where we went wrong.

The Second-Person Plural

A caller once asked if you could use *you'uns,* to which I replied in my characteristically supercilious fashion, "No, I can't, but other people can and do."

You'uns is a common term in certain parts of the United States (and, of course, in Scotland, where it may have originated). I think the more interesting question is whether *you'uns, y'all,* and the urbanized form I'm most used to, *youse,* can be used in the singular or whether they always refer to more than one person.

Time was when English had separate second-person pronouns for singular (*thou, thee, thy, thine*) and plural (*you, ye, your*). There was even a pronoun in Old English called the dual—*yit* or *git*—to indicate that you were addressing two people. But the dual disappeared in Middle English (1100–1500). It was apparently a time when thinking in twos was not fashionable.

Traditional grammatical wisdom says that *y'all* (I am urged by one expert to spell it *ya'll*), *you'uns,* and *youse* are all plural, but I've heard *you all* and *youse* used in reference to a single person. Those few Southerners who admit to singular *y'all* insist it is really a plural used politely for one person. However, some of my correspondents from the Southwest claim it can be a true singular as well. In addition, the existence of "*all y'all*" suggests a need to reinforce the declining plurality of *y'all. You* itself is a plural pronoun which was used politely for the singular and which eventually ousted the singular *thou* during the English Renaissance, so it's not strange to see that pattern continuing with more recent second-person variants.

By the way, we owe the survival of *thou* and *thee,* which have a definitely archaic or old-fashioned flavor, to the influence of the King James translation of the Bible, the English Book of Common Prayer, and the adoption of the pronoun by the seventeenth-century Quakers. Although *thou* is the subject form and *thee* the object form, Modern English speakers who never mix up the subject and object forms of *I, me,* or *she, he,* tend to treat *thee* and *thou* as interchangeable.

An important related issue is whether or not *you guys* can refer to women. As we just saw, *you* is no longer unambiguously singular or plural. This situation led to the rise of clearly marked second person plurals like *y'all.* The newest of these marked plurals is *you guys.* It's increasing in popularity and has been generating a bit of controversy, too. Some people insist that *guy* can only apply to males, while for other folks it is completely gender-neutral, particularly in the plural form, *guys.* What seems to have happened is that, like *man* and compounds formed with man (policeman, Congressman, weatherman), *guys* is yet another masculine term that has come to function as a generic. What is unusual is that it has done so during the exact same era in which we have become increasingly alert to sexism in language. So *man* becomes *person, policeman* becomes *police officer, congressman* becomes *representative,* and *weatherman* becomes *meteorologist.* And some people transmute *guys* into some other more obviously neutral term. But the usage is not uniform: several women who find *guy* to be an unobjectionable, neutral term also report that they can even use the singular *dude* to refer to another woman.

Since *you guys* is informal, occurring mainly in speech (and possibly not in areas where *y'all* is common), it hasn't provoked much comment in the usage guides. But my guess is that as it continues to spread, its significance will be more hotly debated (some of our more recent dictionaries mention the new, gender-neutral sense of *guy*, though only one warns against it). For now, the academy for political correctness has nixed *you guys*, although the person in the street continues to use it.

The Mstery of Ms.

Language goes on despite the worst efforts of either the conservatives or the radicals. The case of *Ms.* offers a perfect illustration.

Ms. has always been treated better by the business community than it has by the literary establishment. But whatever you think of *Ms.*, what seems to be happening is that for an increasing number of college-age women, *Ms.* is becoming not a marriage-neutral title analogous to Mr. but a trendy synonym for *Miss*. Consequently, many of my women students say they are *Ms.* now but intend to become *Mrs.* when they marry. And for a significant subset of these young women, *Ms.* refers not to their peers at all but exclusively to the no-longer-married women of their mothers' generation.

Ms. derives from *Miss*, not from a blend of *Miss* and *Mrs.* as the dictionaries mistakenly claim. It originated from the feminist suggestion in the early part of the century that *Miss* be generalized as the universal feminine title. But, like all language reforms, once it's been set in motion it takes on a life of its own, certainly beyond the control of feminists or English teachers (not that these are mutually exclusive categories). My guess is that the usage of *Ms.* will remain complex and conflicted for some time to come.

Can Women Be Fellows?

I was asked this quite seriously by a (male) graduate school dean whose executive committee was contemplating the backlash that could ensue from awarding fellowships to women. And it's not an entirely silly question, since *fellow* carries primarily a male association.

Indeed, women were so systematically excluded from higher education in the United States that once they started receiving college degrees, in the nineteenth century, some schools (including women's colleges) thought it inappropriate to call female graduates *bachelors* of arts or sciences. There followed a brief flurry of women's degrees, including maid of arts, mistress of arts, sister of arts, and lady literate of arts (this last from St. Andrews University). More recently, some colleges have offered *ovulars* in place of seminars, and one language reformer called for the degree of spinster of arts.

In any case, the dean was not happy with the alternatives: *scholarships* are usually awarded to undergraduates, and *assistantships* usually require teaching or helping a faculty member with research. I'm afraid I had nothing helpful to offer. But I will be pleased to forward your suggestions to the dean, if he's still in office when this book goes to press.

What Is a Waitron?

Continuing with the broad discussion of politically correct language, we come to the question of the *waitron*. Although it sounds like a robot waiter at an Automat, *waitron* is a recently-coined word offering a sex-neutral way of referring to waiters and waitresses. According to the *Random House Webster's College Dictionary*, a *waitron* is "a person of either sex who waits on tables." This definition, the editors claim, derives from a "b[lend] of *waitress* and *neutron*," hardly a sex-neutral etymology. I rather think *waitron* comes from the phrase *waiter on*, and that it is influenced by the suffix *-tron*, which suggests some kind of scientific gizmo.

The *Random House Webster's*, touted by its promoters as well as its critics as the first politically correct, or PC, dictionary, also has an entry for the gender-neutral *waitperson*, which in turn refers us to the usage note for *-person*, where we learn that "the *-person* compounds are used, esp. by the media and in government and business communications, to avoid the *-man* compounds."

Curiously, the *Random House Webster's* has no entry for *wait* as a noun meaning 'waiter/waitress,' although it's a form used frequently in the restaurant biz. The plural is either *waits* or the pseudo-classical *waitri*, which sometimes appears on menus and in want ads. Right now *server* is the most common alternative to the waiter/waitress pair, though it too is missed by the PC dictionary (*server* is defined in the *Merriam-Webster's Collegiate Dictionary*, 10th ed. [1993], as 'one that serves food or drink'). While the *Random House Webster's* provides usage notes for many of its entries, nowhere does it tell us that *waitperson* may be awkward and cumbersome, no evidence is presented that people are identifying themselves as *waits*, or *waitrons* rather than *waiters* and *waitresses*. ("Sure, I'm an actor now, but I'm just doing this until a job as a waitron opens up.")

Language Taboos

A caller told me once that he'd noticed a sharp increase in vulgarity and profanity in the past fifteen years or so. He was also troubled that "a lot of people are using y. k. all the time. I can't actually say this word out loud but *you know* what I mean."

Indeed I knew right away that "y. k." stood for "you know." I routinely survey my students, and anyone else who will sit still long enough, about the aspects of English today they dislike most. I do this because people seem to expect me and all the other language commentators to dislike the English language, or at least to take a dim view of everyone who tries to use it. But I for one don't take a dim view. Not at all. I love nothing better than to collect the variants and innovations of the language that provide my bread and butter. Sure, there's some things I dislike, but not many. But I figure that the people who expect language experts to be negative about their subject must have a lot of negative feelings about English that they need to express. And I don't mind helping them to face their prejudices.

Anyway the "least favorite things" I find in these informal surveys are spelling, obscenity, and *you know*. So if so many people don't like them, why are they so popular? Let's look at the last two now. We'll do spelling in the next chapter.

1. *You know*. The main objection to *you know* is that it is not used literally as a request for confirmation. It doesn't mean, 'Do you know what I mean?' or 'You know very well what I'm talking about,' especially when it occurs frequently. What it is is a filler, like "um" and "er" and "uh" or just plain silence, and it functions to let other participants in a conversation know you aren't done talking yet, but are busy thinking of how to complete your thought. I distinctly remember grade-school teachers warning me against fillers like "um" (this was before the heyday of *you know*, so you know how old I am). But silence isn't always very efficient, since not saying anything is frequently misinterpreted as a signal that you're through talking (a lot

of answering machines have hung up on me in mid-message while I paused to silently rephrase what I wanted to say).

However, as the nearly universal complaining about *you know* indicates, it can be more annoying than being interrupted. People are tempted to respond, "No, I don't know, actually, which is why you are telling me this in the first place, isn't it?"—or they would if they could get a word in edgewise. I had a friend who *you-knowed* in direct proportion to his level of anxiety. When he was, you know, really, you know, nervous, like, the you-know level, would, you know, go off the you-know scale. And when he was calm you could almost think he was normal.

As a filler, *you know* is limited to speech or to the representation of speech in dialogue writing. There is no need for fillers in nonfiction writing since writing is not normally interactive, the way speech often is. With the advent of the computer, however, things may be changing. For example, when I dial up a mainframe from my desktop computer I must keep up a certain level of keyboard activity or the mainframe will assume I'm done and disconnect me. So sometimes, while I'm thinking of what to do next or looking something up in the instruction manual, I stop typing for a while, and **blam,** I'm suddenly off-line with no warning. So to prevent this I am forced to type some nonsense every few minutes, just a meaningless sequence of letters, like this sdfghjkl—to let the mainframe know I'm still working. Soon computers may become as annoyed with this filler as human listeners have become with *you know*.

2. *Taboo.* Obscenity (and profanity, which also troubles lots of my respondents) used to be more of a taboo than it is now. The interesting question here is not whether American society has become so decadent that anything goes, but what is the nature of linguistic taboo? What can we say, what can't we say, what can we only hint at indirectly (through euphemism)? Our discomfort with obscenity indicates that, even if it is more common in public discourse than it used to be, it may still have some secret power, some shock value, some restrictions on its use or its effect (for example, it's still not common in formal speech, still regulated over the airwaves).

We may look as well for its replacement, since the disappearance of one set of taboos may be the signal for the appearance of a new set. There are new taboos arising all the time. The political correctness debate has called attention to a wide variety of labels that may no longer be appropriate in edited writing or polite, formal speech. For example, we don't hear adult women being referred to as girls very much any more, just as we no longer hear adult African American males being called *boy*. So strong are these taboos that one may think twice about calling African American boys *boys*, or even using *girl* to refer to female children. So some years back Garry Trudeau had an enlightened little girl in his *Doonesbury* comic strip announce the birth of her sister to her nursery school class with the words, "It's a woman! A baby woman!"

Some of these new taboos seem appropriate. Labels can be used to demean or insult an audience intentionally. But insult is not always intentional. Labels can reveal the insensitivity of a speaker or writer to an audience, and as always we are forced to consider the consequences of the words we use. It was once appropriate to call African Americans *colored*. Then *negro* and soon thereafter, *Negro*. More recently, *black* and *Black* were labels of choice. And now *African American* is establishing itself (more often without a hyphen than with one). Indians are now *Native Americans*, coopting a nineteenth-century anti-immigrant term referring to those of Western European (but not Irish or German Catholic) ancestry born in the United States. And Eskimos are *Inuit*, though the term *Eskimo* persists in anthropology. And so it goes.

When some large groups manage to air their concerns, smaller groups begin to complain as well. So, writers using *welsh* or *gyp* may get complaints from the Welsh or the Romany. The Society for the Left-Handed will complain that your "left-handed compliments" are doubly insulting (*ambidextrous* offends them as well: it means having two right hands). Being left-handed myself, I have become sensitive to the new, dismissive sense of *lefty*, used by conservatives to refer to ineffective political left-wingers.

The point is this: if you think language taboos are dead in this fast-paced, enlightened postmodern world, survey your married friends to see how many of them have found satisfactory terms of address for their mothers- and fathers-in-law (*mother* and *father* and their variants don't always work with in-laws; first names often don't fill the bill; some people are forced to wait till they make eye contact before they speak to their in-laws). Or just try opening your mouth or starting to type, and see what happens.

Guide to Don'tspeak

There are other taboos, as well, and here we return to the question of political correctness in language, for there is some debate over words that the politically correct don't want anyone else to say. The University of Missouri school of journalism has issued a guide to don'tspeak, a list of words to avoid in newspaper articles, although they call it a "dictionary of cautionary words and phrases."

The Missouri list of no-no's concerns words which might offend people on the basis of race, religion, ethnicity, gender, age, or physical condition. Have we left anyone out? For example, since the terms *Asiatic* and *oriental* are considered offensive by many, we are sensibly told to use *Asian* or *Asian-American* to refer to people from Asia or to Americans of Asian descent, respectively. But the editors also tell us that *Spanish* is not interchangeable with *Mexican, Latino,* or *Hispanic,* which is not altogether true, since *Hispanic* comes from the Latin word for *Spanish* and is commonly used to refer to the language and people of Spain as well as Latin America. Curiously, they don't ban *Latin America,* despite the fact that the name unfairly submerges the native American population beneath the European.

References to skin color are out if the color is yellow, red, or "swarthy," though black and white are acceptable, despite their descriptive inaccuracy. (The Missouri folks don't say it, but *swarthy,* while not much used today, is the term Benjamin Franklin employed to refer to Pennsylvanians of German descent, whom he considered a race apart way back in the eighteenth century.)

We are warned against calling a minority *articulate* since that implies minorities are usually the opposite. On the other hand, it is presumably OK to distinguish between articulate and inarticulate majorities, if we can find any. We are also told to avoid the word *community,* which "implies a monolithic culture in which people act, think and vote in the same way." Thus, there are no more Asian, black, or gay communities, merely "Black residents of a northside neighborhood" and the like. On the other hand the editors decry the use of *banana, coconut,* and *oreo,* which arise within these now-banned communities and refer to Asian-, Mexican-, and African-Americans who have abandoned their culture, and, presumably, their neighborhood as well. I wonder whether the editors regard white culture and neighborhoods as monolithic?

The Missouri editors argue for strict neutrality of expression because "no person or group can appropriately attach judgmental terms to others," though of course their own opinions are judgmental. I agree that one of the basic principles of communication is "Don't alienate your audience." But I have to insist that judging others is something we do all the time—it's a critic's bread and butter, and editors too are supposed to have firm opinions—and masking offensive terms by using euphemisms doesn't always hide a negative connotation or take the sting from an insult.

These lists of expressions to avoid are nothing new. Back in the nineteenth century Edward S. Gould published his proscribed words in the pages of the *New York Post*. Among Gould's banned words were *jeopardize* and *leniency*. He preferred *jeopard* and *lenity*. He was wrong. Gould insisted that *journal* should only refer to a *daily* publication, though I'm sure the folks at the Missouri school of journalism would object, and he argued that the phrase *you are mistaken* can only mean, 'you are misjudged by someone else.' When you are wrong, he insisted, you must use *you mistake*. Again, Gould was mistaken.

Anyway, no matter how much writers try to clean up their act, someone will always take offense at our language. If you use the word *dormitory*, a common enough expression on any college campus, a dorm director will tell you the proper phrase is *residence hall* or even *campus life center*.

Maybe *I'm* wrong, but every time someone tells *me* not to say or write something, I feel this incredible urge to do it anyway. I guess that's how English stays alive, through a community (I don't mean neighborhood) of users articulate enough to create offensive forms of language as well as innocuous ones, and sensitive enough to know when and when not to use them.

Wherein the Author Evades the Question of Whether He Is Politically Correct

Are you *PC*? That's the question bobbing around American campuses today, sometimes as a joke, but all too often in earnest. *PC* is an abbreviation of course, and it can stand for several things, among them the ubiquitous *personal computer*. But we are dealing here with a new sense for *PC*: as it is used in this chapter, it means 'politically correct.'

What does it mean to be politically correct? Well, for some people it has come to mean being left wing, but it is a term with two definitely opposite political spins. The phrase seems to have arisen among American Marxists and refers ironically to those who accept dogma uncritically. Even more ironically, it has been picked up by conservatives as a blanket term referring to anyone slightly left of the far right. For others still, it means something less literally political, like 'standing for what is right on a given issue.' For example, opposing the Styrofoam packaging of fast food is politically correct, or to use the more politically correct term, it is PC, as is reducing sulfur emissions, increasing literacy, protecting rainforests and dolphins, and opposing apartheid and standardized tests. Incidentally, politically correct people are sometimes called *PCPs*, which sounds like something that depletes the ozone layer.

So why is PC a problem? Because political correctness, whether it is spun by the left, the right, or the center, can be too narrow. Judging people by the positions they take on a key issue may be how we sometimes elect our officials, though it's probably not as important as how good they look on television.

But for those of us who remember the McCarthy era, when professors, writers, directors, and entertainers were persecuted for their suspected non-PC leanings, judging people by litmus tests of political correctness, as both extremes of left and right have always done, sends a chill up the spine. A lot of lives were ruined by the insinuations of the junior senator from Wisconsin, the euphemism the media used to refer to Joe McCarthy, and there is a strong sense that although it is the left wing and not the right that has become associated with political correctness today, the PC-ers have now adopted tactics that they once considered reprehensible and immoral.

Here's what happens when political correctness takes the field these days. The controversial head of a well-known university English department suggests that faculty members who are not PC should be kept off university committees. The Dean of Political Correctness at a western university (currently one of the least PC states in the nation) argues that non-PC faculty should not participate in tenure and promotion decisions. And former Reagan administration official Linda Chavez is first invited as a commencement speaker at a southwestern university with a large Latino student body, then has her invitation revoked when students complain that although she is a prominent Latina, she is not PC.

And when the late, very PC Belgian literary theorist Paul de Man is discovered to have written anti-Semitic columns for Nazi-controlled newspapers in occupied Belgium during the late war, his defenders say he didn't mean it because he was always so PC later in life, while his critics suspect that all politically correct theorists are closet collaborationists.

Of course when these things become public the principals, unlike Joe McCarthy, at least have the sense to be embarrassed. Everybody backs down and says, "That's not really what I meant at all," even though they probably did mean exactly what they said under the banner of political correctness: that some faculty members are just not smart enough to judge others, let alone work with them; that Linda Chavez has no business speaking Spanish; and that, like so many others, Paul de Man really did want to get rid of Europe's Jewish population, and when that didn't quite work he embarked on a more promising second career.

Conservative education critics are pushing the idea that political correctness is left wing and that, by implication, the nation's higher education system is dominated by Commie Pinkos (to revive the language of the McCarthy era). Like most charges that colleges are hotbeds of anything besides horticulture, it just doesn't seem to be true. According to a 1991 UCLA survey of more than 35,000 professors, most college instructors fall into the multiple-choice category usually called "none of the above": they are politically middle-of-the-road. Only five percent of the professoriate consider themselves to be "far left," and 0.4 percent are self-described "far right." In contrast, thirty-seven percent consider themselves "liberal" and forty percent identify their politics as "moderate" (*Chronicle of Higher Education* [May 8, 1991], A15).

In its present incarnation, political correctness may be just a flash in the pan, a depressing shorthand for sorting those who are like us from those who are not. But it's always going to be too easy to judge people on single issues, and it will never be politically correct to defend people with unpopular views, or for that matter to attack political correctness.

Am I PC? That, as we used to say as kids, is for me to know and you to find out.

You Spell Potatoe, I Spell Potato

There is a more literal sense for political correctness that surfaced during the 1992 presidential race: it highlights the correctness, or rather the incorrectness, of the language used by the candidates. Vice President Dan Quayle, in the tradition of American vice presidents, didn't generally have a lot to do, so when he did do something it was usually noticed and he usually received a lot of criticism for it. When he complained about a character on a TV sitcom choosing to be a single parent he got a lot of flack. Squaring off loudly for and against the VP's comments were mostly people operating under the delusion that television gives us something to pattern our lives after.

Politically Correct Language

But when Quayle misspelled potato in an elementary school spelling-bee practice, all h-e-double hockey sticks broke loose. Because as we all know, spelling is more important even than television in American life. I mean, spelling counts, doesn't it? Have you ever heard anyone say "Television counts"?

The Vice President put an extra *e* at the end of *potato*. The student speller, just to be polite, added the *e* as well, and promptly lost the bee. Quayl—I'm herewith penalizing him an *e* for an *e* in the Old Testament tradition—blamed the gaffe on an incorrect cue card he had been handed. But that doesn't change the fact that Quayl misspelled potato. The political commentators had a field day with that misspelling, while the educators moaned about the bad example Quayl was setting for American youth, who already have so many *e*'s they don't know what to do with them.

We know that Quayl's nemesis, Murphy Brown, who is rich, tough, has stage hands to change her baby's diapers, and is not even a real person anyway, will survive single parenthood because it's all in the script. But not knowing how to spell *potato* may have proved fatal to the career of the Vice President, who was born with silver place settings for twelve in his mouth and has probably never had to spell anything in his life.

The message the VP brought to the nation is not what some people claimed: that spelling is important and he can't do it, so he really must've gotten through law school on family influence. The message is that true power rests not in the mind but the pocketbook. If spelling *is* so important, Quayl can pay somebody else to do it for him.

The rich and the powerful don't carry cash. They don't know what scanners are in grocery stores. And they have someone else write everything they say and, of course, check the spelling. If they're caught short, they borrow a dollar from someone in the entourage, or they borrow an *e*.

If you dig into the history of the potato you will find a bushel of spellings, including the one Quayl backed. In one of its earliest incarnations—if a vegetable can be said to have an incarnation—the word began with a *b*, not a *p*. *Potatoe* with an *e* occurs as recently as the mid-nineteenth century, among other places, in the writings of the great naturalist Charles Darwin. If anyone knew how to spell a species, it was Darwin. And we all know that potatoes have eyes, though they never appear in the spelling and so must be considered silent.

But the silent *e* in *potato* went out with the Paperwork Reduction Act, a federal statute aimed at reducing the number of vowels in the language to an acceptable level. No doubt the Vice President was confused because there is an *e* in *toe*, the little digit that wiggles at the end of your foot and rhymes with *potato*, and because there is an *e* in the plural—*potatoes*. Also, a lot of English words end in a silent *e*, including his own name. In this case, however, it was Quayl, and not the *e*, that should have been mute.

The Al and I

Continuing our discussion of politically correct language, by which I don't mean whether you should call waiters and waitresses "waitrons," but whether political figures can use language correctly to begin with, the matter of Vice President Quayl's spelling was quickly obscured by the Democrats' assault on the English pronoun system. Bill Clinton asked Americans to give "Al Gore and I a chance."

The question is, is this really wrong? Usage critics, generally a surly lot, call for "me" when the pronoun is in object position. But "I" is common enough in constructions like "between you and I."

People who don't ever say "between you and I" find it objectionable and ungrammatical; people who use it as a matter of course don't see what all the fuss is about. The classic example of the so-called misuse comes from Shakespeare's *Merchant of Venice*, where Antonio writes to Bassanio, "All debts are cleared between you and I."

Now Clinton, who is no stranger to controversy, was caught in the same pronoun snafu that confounded Shakespeare. Tabloids all across America aimed their telephoto lenses at Clinton's grammar. Family values were once again threatened. But dragging Clinton's pronouns through the mud did not change his or anybody else's behavior.

Is "Al and I" really wrong? Purists insist it is, but like other uses that have been labeled as "errors" it is spreading despite two centuries of eradication efforts. Linguists, whose job it is to analyze the situation rather than to judge it, can't come up with a satisfactory explanation of the "between you and I" phenomenon. Some see it as a hypercorrection, a reaction to our being told as children not to say "Her and me went to the store." Others claim that since "between you and I" only occurs when the pronoun follows "and," the conjunction is somehow at fault. Still other experts find in the construction evidence that English pronouns no longer have distinct subject and object forms, that pronoun declension itself is declining to the point where any pronoun, singular or plural, masculine or feminine, subject or object, can appear anyplace in a sentence. There is considerable support for this last position.

In any case, objective "I" has been popping up ever since Shakespeare's day, and it is not found only among the lower orders, but in the language of people who are generally considered not simply literate, but literarily correct, people who never said anything like "Her and me went to the Rialto." Their language has always been regarded as otherwise standard and they wouldn't be caught dead saying "Give we a chance" or "Give it to I." Besides, English wasn't even a school subject in Shakespeare's day. No one would have said to him, "Watch thou thy pronouns" unless they were teaching him Latin.

Why people use objective "I" is anybody's guess, but it seems to have become an idiom (idioms don't have to follow the normal laws of grammar), like the more generally tolerated subjective "me" of "It's me." But it is an idiom many people disallow. In any case, like misspelled words, objective "I" will continue to occur in the language of the grammatically law-abiding. Both set off some people's radar detectors. And both will bring forth the summons of the language police.

Was Dan Quayle's orthography a graver error than Bill Clinton's pronouns? It was an election year. Ultimately, the voters were the ones to decide.

First Lady

We elected a new president just in time for the nation to face yet another language crisis. Before the election, the issue was whether you could spell potato with an *e*, and whether you could get away with "giving Al and I a chance." The voters decided that you can do the second, not the first, but to no one's surprise, the language crisis just won't go away. It's the one thing you can't blame on twelve years of Republican administration.

The question facing us after the 1992 election was what title to give Hillary Clinton. According to some observers *Ms.* Clinton is just too "modren" to be called the "First Lady," the traditional appellation given to the president's spouse.

Lady is a fairly conflicted term in American English. In British English it is the feminine equivalent of *lord,* and though the pair originally meant something like 'loaf-kneader' and 'loaf-guardian,' they both denote persons of high social status. *Lady* also parallels *gentleman,* and in the nineteenth century the British complained that Americans used *lady* indiscriminately to refer to any woman at all. Nowadays people use it as a euphemism because *woman* often seems too blunt or too sexual a word to refer to female human beings. And *lady* has been further tainted with the sense of inferiority or second-class status in such expressions as *lady doctor, lady lawyer,* and *lady novelist.* No self-respecting American feminist uses *lady,* with its suggestion of women on pedestals and watercress sandwiches.

But if *First Lady* is inappropriate in the Year of the Woman, what are the alternatives? One political columnist, Anna Quindlen, led off by calling Hillary Clinton the *First Woman,* a term which, to me, refers not to a presidential wife but to Eve, or maybe the character in the Navajo origination story. No, *First Woman* just doesn't work for me, as the salespeople say.

Neither does *First Spouse,* the term we will inevitably try out when (not if, when) the president's significant other is of the masculine persuasion. And that term, like *First Wife,* is marred by the fact that it suggests there have been subsequent spouses.

Of course since English is a language of infinite variety, with a large inventory of synonyms, there are other terms to choose from: how about *presidentess*, a word advocated by Sarah Josepha Hale, the self-described *editress* of *Godey's Ladies Book*, the leading nineteenth-century women's magazine? Hale wanted to make women who did things more visible in our vocabulary as well as our society, so in the 1860s she coined the term *presidentess* to refer to the wife of the president (remember at the time that women couldn't vote, so there was not much chance of a woman being the actual president). Hale also favored such feminines as *janitress, professoress, teacheress,* and *doctress*, terms describing women doing real work, not just serving as decorations for their husbands. But Hale was more successful in influencing the world of women's fashion with her magazine than the world of women's words: *presidentess* never did catch on.

Feminine terms like *authoress* and *poetess* are far from fashionable at the moment, so I think we can rule out reviving *presidentess*. When the *Chicago Tribune* called me after the election to ask what term I thought would win the name-Hillary-Rodham-Clinton Sweepstakes, I couldn't see much competition for the traditional *First Lady.* Anyway, Hillary Clinton was already referring to herself as First Lady at least a month before the swearing in. She chose to revise not her title but her name, adding Rodham so that she would appear more businesslike, more presidential.

But so far as titles go, I don't much like *First Lady* either, and, finally, I've come up with the answer. What's the most popular, politically correct word to include women as well as men when we want to play down the role of gender and avoid the generic masculine? It's *person*, of course. *Chairperson. Salesperson. Anchorperson. Spokesperson.* Hillary Rodham Clinton should be the *First Person*. It's an all-purpose title, quintessentially neutral, and when Hillary becomes president, Bill will be the *First Person*.

And if we ever have a president who is not married, she (or he) will be the *First Person, Singular.* As a grammarian, I should have had it on the tip of my tongue.

8 Spelling Counts

Question: "Are you my English teacher?"
Dr. Grammar: Actually, this isn't a question I got on the air or in the mail. Nonetheless, it is a question I was asked way back in 1974, while riding the subway in New York on my way to a class I was teaching at City College.

A young man came up to me and asked, "Are you my English teacher?" New Yorkers normally don't reply when someone on the subway speaks to them. Instead, feigning interest in their newspaper, they check anxiously for the nearest exit. In extreme cases, they shoot first and ask questions later, which I guess isn't all that different from what teachers do, figuratively speaking. But the young man looked harmless so I told him no, I wasn't his English teacher, and he moved on.

He could have been right. I was, after all, *an* English teacher, only not his. Obviously I looked like an English teacher, whatever we are supposed to look like.

This incident came back to me in the Spring of 1992, when I judged the annual regional spelling bee in central Illinois, where I have been an English teacher for quite a while, and a man came up to me and announced that I had been *his* English teacher some twenty years before. He looked vaguely familiar, having aged a couple of decades, and his name was strange to my ear, but I was sure he had been my student after he recalled details of the summer writing class I had inflicted on him. He was now an English teacher himself, I assume through no fault of mine, and his daughter was competing in the bee. He proceeded to describe a new method for teaching writing he was using in the high school where he works. And his question was, what did I think of it?

While it is sobering to be an English teacher and have a stranger on a train mistakenly accost you as his English teacher, it is more sobering still to hear a former student turned teacher ask you to approve a way of teaching that you yourself have always denounced as ineffective and possibly immoral as well.

For writing teachers are pretty adamant about the good ways and bad ways of getting the job done. So, when this former student described a brand-new, rigid, mechanical, surefire drill for following one sentence with another, a method designed to pervert, thwart, and deaden the writing process, but one which he clearly regarded as the cutting edge of the blunted knife of instruction, I'm afraid I was a little ungracious, maybe even impolite.

I've always approached writing as an organic, confused, messy process resistant to formulaic description. I told him I would never teach writing the way he did, as a recipe: do this worksheet, do that exercise, just add words, and poof, instant prose. I knew I was doing the wrong thing, telling him this, but I couldn't stop. My students, like my children, will come to their own conclusions about how to run their lives and other people's. They will do things differently, no matter what I say. If I give them the freedom to be wrong, I have to expect that sometimes they will make mistakes.

I also knew these kinds of pieties about children and students were nonsense, or at least that's what I told myself as—sounding like everyone's stereotype of an English teacher—I plunged ahead to revile my former student's method, which was no doubt encouraged by his curriculum supervisors as a stimulating and productive solution to the problem of literacy in the schools, but which I condemned as uncreative and stultifying, definitely a step backward, an obstacle in the path of reading and writing, an effort which I would grade as a failure. Or words to that effect.

Fortunately, like the student he must have been during that long hot prairie summer twenty years ago, he didn't hear me. Convinced that he was doing the right thing by his own students, and convinced that I approved, that I might even be proud, he thanked me, and the conversation shifted to his daughter's spelling. She didn't win that day, but she was a good speller, and we were both proud of her effort.

As school lets out and the prospect of another in the endless series of hot prairie summers yawns before me, I wonder for a moment whether my students this year heard anything I said to them. Or if they even remember, now that finals are over, who I am. I know why I feel this way. Not because of an incident at a spelling bee, or an encounter on the IRT. All year long, teachers complain about students. All year long, we look forward to the summer. Yet each year we feel such loss when summer finally comes.

Question: Does Spelling Count?

The answer to that is a definite "sometimes." There's one place where it does, almost always: the spelling bee.

Take a chess tournament, with its clash of sheer intellect. Add to it a dash of Little League, pitting America's youth against screaming parents and scowling coaches. Mix in the luck of the lottery. Top it all off with the commercial hype of Bowling for Dollars, and what you have is the greatest of all American contests, the spelling bee.

For several years now I have served as a judge of the regional spelling bee, televised locally and regularly on a Saturday morning in April, preempting "The Mental Misadventures of Cartoon Mutant Turtles" and part of the network baseball pre-game show. The spelling bee tests the ability of school children to spell such rare words as *numnah,* a kind of saddle blanket; *sacciform,* which means 'pouch-like'; and *procacity,* meaning 'disrespect.' The winner goes on to meet some two hundred other regional winners in the national competition in Washington, D.C., where they will be asked to spell words even more hideously obscure than *laloplegia* and *forbivorous.*

Unlike "The Price Is Right" or "The Iran-Contra Hearings," the spelling bee is not all greed and spectator sport. We are in there with the contestants for the long haul, letter by letter. Once they start a word, there is no turning back. You can cut the tension at the spelling bee with a knife. Our emotions are wracked with the joy of a successful *dacquoise, newspaporial,* and *nephelometer;* we are tortured by a missed *decumbent, intertriginous,* or *stentorophonic.*

I am truly impressed with the ability of these young people—their average age is about twelve—to subdue the unruly monster of English spelling, whose complexities have been the bane of generations of scholars. Our greatest writers had trouble with spelling. Jane Austen misspelled *friendship,* the title of her first novel, and Shakespeare seldom spelled his name the same way twice. Many an English teacher is helpless without a dictionary or a computer spell checker (by the way, my own spell checker has none of the spelling-bee words listed above in its data base). So if they're so smart, why can't they spell?

We don't really know why some people spell well and others don't. Good memory helps, as does a knowledge of word origins. I would like to think that reading and writing help as well. But good spellers don't necessarily know what their words mean. And, as I mentioned earlier in this book, spelling-bee winners are not known for their success in the literary world.

It is notoriously difficult to teach a poor speller to spell: for most of us, memorizing lists of words works only in the short run. The day after the spelling test, it's back to the dictionary. Even using a word often is no guarantee that you won't spell it creatively: I still have to check the *e*'s in precede and proceed. Does practice have an *s* or a *c*?

The spelling bee reflects the emphasis we place on correct spelling in America, and it is good publicity for the English language, which can always do with a boost. The spelling bee is a diversion, albeit a very serious one for those involved, present company included. The spelling bee is proof that spelling counts. But despite the hype that surrounds it, spelling is, at best, a superficial language skill. We cannot confuse spelling competence with true literacy, which counts even more. That is only gained through reading and writing, and not the memorization of lists.

But Does Spelling Count?

In my answer to the previous question, I stated that spelling, unlike quiz shows, didn't involve greed. I was wrong. At the height of spelling fever season, one of the cable television channels ran an ad for a spelling bee you could play at home by phone, with cash prizes awarded to contestants who could correctly spell a certain number of words by pushing the buttons fast enough on their touchtone phones. Quite a feat if you can do it, since there are three letters on each button, and no *q* or *z*. Much like knocking down the heavily weighted bottles in the baseball throw at the county fair.

So spelling does count, after all. That great American poet T. S. Eliot—who hailed from St. Louis but spent most of his life in London trying to become British—anyway, Eliot called April the cruellest month and I think he did that because it's the month of the regional spelling bee.

According to Eliot, April is the cruellest month because it mixes memory and desire, and what better way to mix them than in a heated contest which pits the ability to memorize the trivial eccentricities of English spelling against the desire to win the title of Mr. or Ms. American Orthography?

Americans are not the only ones to put a high value on the ability to spell. France held the finals of its spelling championship last December. Instead of contestants taking turns spelling words they've never heard before and will never use again, spelling till they drop, the more than two hundred French finalists, only half of whom are actually native French speakers, gathered at the National Library in Paris and copied a dictation read by the French television equivalent of Alistair Cooke.

The person who writes the dictation making the fewest number of mistakes is declared the winner. In case of a tie, contestants copy an additional set of fiendishly difficult sentences. And there are plenty of opportunities for mistakes. Not only is French spelling, like its English counterpart, different from the way actual words are spoken, but French writing is complicated by a variety of accents and silent letters added to make words agree in gender and number.

If anything, spelling counts more in France than it does in the United States. You can't pass the baccalaureate, the national examination students must take to get any sort of decent job, unless you spell faultlessly. The pass rate on that test is a mere forty percent. For the first time in its history, the French spelling contest, which was televised live on prime-time TV, produced a perfect, mistake-free paper. It was written by a classics professor from Strasbourg, a city where German, not French, is the street language.

If the French government has its way, spelling will count even more in the future. A law is in the works to reform French spelling—to take out some of the nastier accents and forms of silent agreement—but like all governmental proposals, what seems like a gift often turns out to be a punishment. The new law will make spelling mistakes even more fatal: misspell a word on a check and it will bounce; misspell something on your tax return and you can kiss that refund good-bye.

Such a law would certainly be a hardship here in the States. It's bad enough that we're expected to make sure the numbers on our tax returns add up. Think of the chaos if we had to remember *i* before *e* except when carrying the *e-i-g-h-t*. Maybe T. S. Eliot was doing his taxes when he wrote his deathless lines. What can you expect from a man whose name spelled backwards almost spells *toilets*? But almost, in the spelling bee, is not good enough.

The Daemon Spell Checker

Spelling checkers are a lot like calculators. Just as you can buy pocket calculators that will add and subtract and multiply and divide and take square roots and do percents and a whole slew of what once were messy arithmetic operations, you can now buy little battery-operated machines to spell everything for you.

Does the availability of these pocket spellers signal the end of Western civilization as we know it? Should they be banned from the classroom? Years back, some math teachers wanted to ban calculators

Spelling Counts

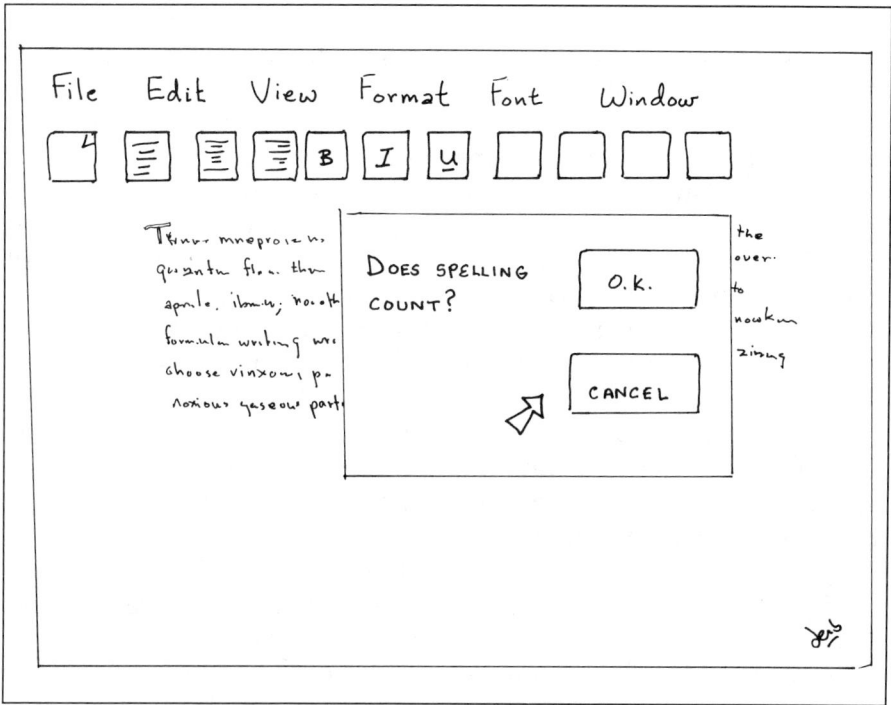

because they felt that if students relied on them they would never master arithmetic. But today calculators are everywhere, and students seem no better or worse at arithmetic than they ever were. I learned to add and subtract the old-fashioned way, memorizing tables. And I could never get my checkbook to balance until I started using a calculator. I don't think I could do my taxes without one. My accountant uses one, and he's certainly good with numbers.

Spelling, like math, is considered a basic skill. And you hear a lot about the basics nowadays. They are something we are always admonished to get back to, which of course assumes that they were something we were once at. Just what are the basics, anyway? Well, for one thing, the basics are always plural. You never see a basic out there all by itself, only basics. "The basics" travel in packs, like wild animals.

For some time now the cry among educators has been "Get back to the basics." I imagine a lone teacher holding a chair and a whip, surrounded by a bunch of snarling beasts, and the teacher is crying, "Get back, get back to the basics!"

So what is a basic, when it's at home? Well, in the area of language, one of the basics for many people has always been spelling. It's an important school subject, and a difficult one as well. And as such, it's something that students have always feared. Hence their perennial question, "Does spelling count?"

But spelling is not so much a basic as it is a convention of behavior, a kind of language etiquette we use to separate the educated from the uneducated, the tamed from the wild. Knowing how to spell well is the equivalent of knowing which fork to use for fish. Though it functions for us as a sign of good writing and clear thinking, it is neither of these. Spelling is a test not of creativity or intelligence but of rote memory.

Now I know that sounds mighty controversial, coming from an English teacher. Put that way, spelling is not an essential of language but a kind of frill or window dressing. The sort of thing you can now use a computer to take care of.

At the university, when we first started to teach writing using word processors, we didn't tell our students there was a spell checker they could use. We feared that students would rely on them instead of dictionaries. But the hackers found the spell checkers anyway.

You can't stop spelling machines. The question is, should you want to? My spelling is probably a lot better than my arithmetic. That's one reason I became a writer instead of an accountant. But I find a spell checker is essential when I write, because my typing and proofreading skills are weak, and my memory is like a steel trap rusted open.

Spelling machines are not the end of literacy. Quite the opposite: their popularity indicates the value we still place on accurate spelling. Perhaps the only thing a spelling machine will signal the end of is spelling bees, which will become more anachronistic than they already are.

A Language Museum

If you've ever wondered where dead words go, here's the answer. They go to the spelling bee. Take, for example, Spelling Bee VII (I've started to number them, like the Super Bowl). Since the local station televising the event isn't used to much home-grown programming other than the news, the set they devised, a backdrop of fourteen large bees who looked like they had *not* been drawn by Walt Disney, fell down halfway through the show, right between the two *m*'s in *summinct,* though the youngster who was spelling the word didn't skip a beat.

Since the hard words to spell tend to be so unusual, the spelling bee offers the casual observer a trip through a museum of English. We abandon the street language that accompanies our daily lives to enter a quiet place housing the old, the strange, the rare word, the word on loan from another collection. We look and we listen. We do not touch.

The other spelling-bee judges, a former reporter for the TV station and the advertising manager for the sponsoring newspaper, share with the audience a sense of goodwill and a general inability to spell. One judge complained to me that so many of the words weren't even English. There were words like *brasserie, brochette,* and *pourboire* from the French; *weltpolitik* from German; *meshummad* from Hebrew; *cabasa, mazagran,* and *hacienda* from the Spanish; even *kielbasa* and *salami* from the sausage. To which the person responsible for choosing the words responded defensively: "But they're English too—they're in the dictionary."

The presence of so many "foreign" words in English attests to our language's borrowing power. After all, English didn't come to have the largest vocabulary of any language on earth by practicing isolationism. Long before the British Empire reached out to cover the planet, English was already reaching out and absorbing foreign words or coining homegrown words on classical models. That's why we have words like *octarchy,* 'government by eight rulers'; *plumbeous,* 'lead-like'; *cassideous,* 'helmet-shaped'; and *tessaraglot,* 'having four languages.' Not that there's much call for these words, or ever was. *Tessaraglot* was used but once before the spelling bee, to indicate a four-language bible; *cassideous* is a technical term confined to plant description; *octarchy* refers to the eight kingdoms of Anglo-Saxon England. Only *plumbeous* has a more extensive history, though it is not a common word today: we don't use plumbeous and aplumbeous gasoline, we use leaded and unleaded. Anyway, the "foreignness" of many English words offers one of the many pitfalls of our spelling system.

It is a general principal that the less common the word, the less easy it will be to spell. Spelling-bee words, then, normally fall into the category of the less than common. How many times do you find yourself saying *nemoral,* which means 'pertaining to or living in groves or woods'—let alone writing it or reading it? Or *limacine,* which means 'slimy, like a snail'? *Morigeration* is not something you need more of in the summer. It means 'obsequiousness, deference to superiors,' and was used occasionally, though without much enthusiasm, for a couple of centuries. And *phalacrosis*, which means 'baldness,' isn't even found in the *Oxford English Dictionary*, let alone in ads for hair restoration.

If the spelling bee is a museum, are the spellers then its curators? I'm not about to argue that knowledge is worthless unless it is immediately useful, but it seems to me that rewarding nine-year-olds for spelling words like *tauromachy*—whose meaning they cannot even begin to guess at (it's 'bullfighting,' in case you wondered) is a little bit like training seals. You are getting empty, reflex knowledge, not critical problem-solving skills or even aesthetic enjoyment. On the other hand, maybe their time *is* better spent memorizing the spelling of hard words than playing video games—spelling is certainly cheaper. And the kind of spelling prowess tested in the bee is surely rare enough to warrant putting it on display.

But I still fail to see how spelling a word whose meaning you fail to grasp does anything to "increase vocabularies and develop correct usage of the language," two of the three goals of the spelling bee. The third, obviously enough, is to improve spelling skills, and I'm convinced that the best way to do that is not to memorize lists but to read and write as much as possible.

So why, you might wonder, if I insist on questioning the validity of spelling bees, do I continue to judge the event? I love the fact that once a year, a local television station is happy to interrupt network cartoons to spend an hour listening to the English language in all its glory. And frankly, I'm hooked on the spectacle. Besides, the spelling bee has some educational value for its participants: you know they come away from it and for the rest of their lives they'll be able to spell the word they lost on, or the word that won them the match.

9 What's the Latest Word?

New Words for 1988

It was January again, and just when you'd thought the roundups of the year gone by were done, there was another: the best words of 1988. Word collectors, spearheaded by dictionary giant Merriam-Webster of Springfield, Massachusetts, collect and analyze each year's lexical innovations and attempt to rule on what is ephemeral and what is here to stay—and so we were treated to a list of something like the year's ten best-dressed words.

Want to know what was at the top? According to the harmless drudges of Springfield, *computer virus* lead off as the critics' choice for number one logo. You should all know by now what a computer virus is: a program designed to infiltrate and reproduce itself in host computer systems. Benign viruses simply slow computers down or flash silly messages like "Twang your magic twanger, froggy" on your screen. Malign viruses actually destroy data and threaten national security. The virus program is transmitted when an affected disk is placed in a computer; the virus can then infect clean disks inserted into the machine and pass it on.

Author Susan Sontag traces the virus metaphor to the AIDS epidemic. The threat of computer viruses has led to calls to end disk promiscuity, to practice "safe" computer use like "safe" sex. According to Sontag, had it not been for AIDS, we would be talking about these nasty computer programs in the metaphors of international terrorism instead.

What else was big in vocabulary in '88? Well, there was *colorization*, the computerized tinting of black-and-white movies to make them palatable to today's television viewers. There were screams when Ted Turner broadcast his colorized *Casablanca,* and B&W fans have gone to court to attempt to block the release of colorized versions of some of the great films of the '40s. Federal law has since designated a number of films as something like national monuments. They can no longer be edited for broadcast or rental (which brings up the interesting question of whether or not a movie like *The Wizard of Oz* must be shown on TV without commercial breaks).

What are some of the other hit words of 1988? Another list supplied by John Algeo, new-word fiend from the University of Georgia, lists *postmodern,* a word gaining strength as *modern* loses its ability to refer to the present. Here at the university we talk of postmodernism in architecture and in literature. But the word is clearly breaking new ground: a local rental unit advertises *postmodern apartments*.

And there's *shock radio*—that's not our mild-mannered language commentator or even the abrasive mechanical brothers who discuss automobile maintenance on National Public Radio, it's outright audience insult and off-the-wall scatology, the kind of radio that needs a large metropolitan market to sustain an audience willing to be beaten about the ears each night by the *shock jock*.

Then there's *couch potato,* which seems to be making the shift from slang to standard, and *microwaveable*—more and more foods and utensils are microwaveable; I'm waiting for the marketplace to turn all these new words into a single product: a microwaveable beer and potato chip couch potato colorized TV dinner. It's so postmodern. In the meantime, I'm hoping it's true that Ted Turner plans to colorize those monochrome "M*A*S*H" reruns broadcast every night on one of our local stations.

A Liberal Education

It might surprise you that the word *liberal* is relatively new to politics, and its current rejection by politicians of every political stripe suggests its usefulness in that arena may be over, at least for now. In some sense, then, this commentary may be a semantic obituary.

Liberal began life with meanings that are radically different from its present ones. The adjective *liberal* comes from the Latin meaning 'free' and was at first the opposite of *servile,* or 'servant-like.' Originally, the *liberal arts* were those subjects studied by free citizens, the well-born and financially independent. In contrast, the *mechanical arts* were subjects suited to the rest of us poor stiffs who have to work for a living. Now all that has changed, and it is common in our society to think of the liberal arts as a ticket to poverty, while success can only be gained through a practical, professional education.

Another meaning of *liberal* is 'generous': a *liberal offer* is bountiful, *liberal terms* are easy ones, and, by extension, a person of *liberal proportions* is fat. The word also meant unrestrained, frequently in the negative sense: Shakespeare, for example, speaks of a *liberal villain.* A *liberal interpretation* is a loose one, the opposite of a literal or strict construction. *Liberal* also developed the sense 'open-minded, free from prejudice or bigotry.'

It was not until the early nineteenth century that *liberal* developed its political sense in England, where it meant favoring constitutional change and government reform, specifically, getting the government off the people's backs. Liberals opposed the Conservatives, who sought to maintain the status quo, an aristocratic, unrepresentative government rather than a democratic one.

At first, then, *conservatives* were the big-government folks, and *liberals* were about as right-wing as today's *libertarians*. In American politics, *liberal* kicked around during the nineteenth century, but really became prominent with the New Deal and World War II. Soon thereafter, the word began its long decline. In the 1960s the liberal Adlai Stevenson defined a liberal as someone with both feet planted firmly in the air. Nowadays, however, *liberal* has become a dirty word, often prefaced by *knee-jerk, bleeding-heart,* or, most recently, *card-carrying*.

Today's political liberals flee from the label because it implies ineffectuality at best and subversive activity at worst. After all, *card-carrying* was initially used in the 1930s to refer to fellow-traveling American Communists. But according to William Safire's *Political Dictionary*, when red-baiting Wisconsin Senator Joe McCarthy made *card-carrying* a household expression in the 1950s, the first extension of the term by political commentators was not to liberals at all but to *card-carrying, rock-ribbed Republicans* like Senator Robert Taft and Richard Nixon. In fact, Safire maintains that the term cannot properly be applied to liberals at all.

Clearly, like most political words, it is difficult to pin *liberal* down to a specific meaning. Perhaps that's because language is always changing. But I suspect the real reason is because it's impossible to pin down the politicians behind the words.

We may not have *liberal* to kick around in politics anymore, but as the resident grammarian of WILL-AM, at the University of Illinois, I take comfort in the fact that grammar, while it doesn't always bring in the bucks, is still one of the seven liberal arts.

The Best Words of the Decade

Somebody once tried to convince me that the decade of the '80s would not end until December 31, 1990, just as the twentieth century would not end with the close of 1999, a technicality which forced Arthur C. Clarke to call his popular novel-of-the-future *2001*, not *2000*. But I decided to go ahead with this piece at the end of 1989 anyway.

After all, when the sands of 1899 ran out, the *London Times* ran a sidebar reminding its readers that the century wouldn't turn for yet another year, while a front-page banner headline confidently told those same readers that the long-awaited twentieth century was here at last. Which goes to show you that Lewis Carroll was right when he had Humpty Dumpty tell Alice that words mean exactly what we choose them to mean, neither more nor less.

When we talk about the '80s, we mean the ten-year span, or decade, between 1980 and 1989, and when we discuss the 1900s we mean the one hundred years between 1900 and 1999. So the 1900s and the twentieth century do not coincide exactly. That's not a problem for most of us, though every time a year ends in a nine, purists come out to tell us not to start the party yet. If you're a millenarian waiting in a tree for the world to end I can see why a more precise method of dating things would be useful for you.

Anyway, to get back to the subject, which is the five best words of the '80s—sort of like the ten best films—here is my personal list, in reverse order, of course, to keep up the suspense.

Number 5: *microwaveable*. A holdover from 1988, this little word has come to symbolize all that is good and true in American society—it is the universal seal of approval, and I see it as one day replacing *kosher*, in its extended sense of 'permissible; OK,' for example, "Diverting funds earmarked for low-income housing is not microwaveable."

4. *Euro-*. Anything to do with design was *Euro-* in the 1980s, as if after Michelangelo and Pierre Cardin no one else has a lock on style. Cars, coffeepots, and dollars were *Euro-*. A book on economics, not geology, predicted the *Euroquake*. A spy novel referred to the continental homeless as *Eurotrash*. And of course there is *EuroDisney*. How long before plastic surgeons start offering the *Euronose*?

3. *Liberal*. Now *liberal* is probably one of the most ambiguous words of the decade. When liberal regimes are established in Eastern Europe this is seen as political enlightenment, but at home *liberal* is associated with flags on the floor, urological artwork, and urban education, three things that American society finds embarrassing.

2. The first runner-up, which will take the place of the number one word should that word not be able to fill out its term, is *awesome*. This word needs no introduction. It is the superlative of superlatives,

and as such it is also totally meaningless. To label something as *awesome,* or even better, *totally awesome,* is to say nothing about it. A synonym for *awesome* is *excellent,* as in "That bar mitzvah party was really excellent." Yuppies say *excellent* when they mean *awesome.*

1. But the winner of the word of the '80s competition is *biodegradable.* Now here's a word that reminds us all of our mortality. *Bio* means 'life,' after all, and to me *biodegradable* is not plastics that claim to disintegrate in landfills but the big sleep, the great leveler, the equalizer, the grimmest of reapers. Like all award-winning words, *biodegradable* is infinite in its possibilities: "That movie was totally biodegradable." "The Romanians have instituted a biodegradable form of government."

Even the word *biodegradable* is biodegradable. It has an estimated half-life of ten years, after which it becomes *biodeg.* In twenty years there's barely a *bio* left. In the year 2000 I'll give you my list of the best words of the twentieth century. If I waited till 2001, there'd be no one left to care.

New Words of 1990

With the turn of the year from 1990 to 1991, at least on the Gregorian calendar, I again took a few moments to reflect on the most important words of the year gone by. The year 1990 was a big year for history: iron curtains tumbled; sandstorms roiled; savings and loans, bellying up with abandon, reminded their depositors that, outside the movies, life was not necessarily all that wonderful.

1990 was a big one for English as well, with new words and new meanings testing the marketplace as usual, and with a surprising number of old words that filed for Chapter 11. Here's my list of some of the most active words of that year:

Green—always an important symbol in our language, *green* has meant everything from 'new' and 'innocent' to 'envious' to 'rolling in dough,' and now it means 'environmentally aware' as well. *Green* used to conjure up images of banks, or maybe vegetables, but now industrial polluters are wrapping themselves in the green flag. Even Styrofoam is becoming green, according to the producers of *biodegradable plastics,* though the antiStyrofoam lobby finds that phrase a contradiction in terms, another example of word pollution. Spray a little of the new biodegradable insecticides on a little pest like a medfly or your neighbor's pit bull, who seems to have left his teeth in your green plastic recycling bucket, and the poison metabolizes without a trace by the time your neighbor gets home from work.

And speaking of *green*, let's not forget its antonym, *chemical*. Yes, that's right, *green* and *chemical* are opposites, because *chemical* has come to mean 'anything that's bad for you.' Remember the advertising slogan "Better Living Through Chemistry"? Now it's "Don't eat that, it's got chemicals," because we're convinced that chemicals will kill us. Of course people are made up entirely of chemicals, but that's just one more argument against cannibalism so far as the right-to-a-chemical-free environmentalists are concerned. And then there are those who pretend their chemicals are green, like ECOLAB Pest Control, an outfit whose truck cruises my neighborhood regularly, and whose employees wear heavy coveralls, space helmets, and thick rubber gloves: don't tell me they're using water in those spray tanks.

Chemical leads me to the big dud of 1990, *cold fusion*, the empty promise that thermonuclear energy would soon be produced in every American kitchen. The fizzling of cold fusion, an embarrassment to the two chemists who initially touted it, proved a relief to bomb squads all over the country who would have to dispose of the radioactive waste if this more literal way of nuking dinner became widespread.

So we won't have *cold fusion* to kick around any more. And speaking of duds, this brings us to another short-lived 1990 word, one you've probably forgotten already, *peace dividend:* that's the windfall savings we were supposed to reap when the *iron curtain*, a term coined by Winston Churchill in the '40s, got razed, and the Cold War got freeze-dried. *Peace dividend* surfaced briefly after the Vietnam War, then resumed its hibernation until recently. *Cold War* too is a term that has gone on *hiatus* (itself a relatively new bit of jargon used in the television industry to refer to a series that the critics love but no one wants to watch). Anyway, the less said about the peace dividend in these times of renewed confrontation and sandblasted budgets, the better.

Looking ahead, it's hard to predict what the big words will be by the turn of the century. But we can hope that some familiar words will become insolvent. Here is one set of new word resolutions: that the sand trap of the Middle East and the bamboo curtain will join the iron curtain and the Berlin Wall in oblivion; that hot fusion will become as defused as cold fusion; and that the next big words to pass from current events into history will be *AIDS* and *apartheid*. It could happen. And they could tap Jimmy Stewart for the lead in the movie version of the story of the Savings and Loan debacle.

The Best Words of 1991

If 1990 was a big year for political events influencing our vocabulary, then 1991 proved a real corker. We started out the year with two variations on the shifting sands, *Desert Shield* and *Desert Storm*, immortalized on T-shirts, though perhaps less crucial to the annals of military history than we initially anticipated, and we waited in vain for *the mother of all battles*, as we look now without much hope for the mother of all new words.

For the new words of 1991 were not so much innovations as they were obvious revisions of older words. Where *wannabe* was a powerful force in the me-decade of the '80s, *used-to-be* became the operative concept in the roaring '90s. 1991 was a year of *formers* and *posts*. At one end of the year we saw *East Germany* become the *former East Germany*, or *the former GDR*, and eventually, Eas*tern* Germany, while at the other end of the annual cycle the *Soviet Union* became *the former Soviet Union*, an event which has proved jolting to those who for years have been reminded by political purists to say *Soviet Union*, not *Russia*. The economic impact of this change on the map-making industry is only now beginning to be felt as globe after globe finds its way to the clearance aisle in the discount stores. Just what will become of "the former Soviet Union" is still unclear, though some Soviet watchers are betting it will simply become Russia once again. How long it will take Russia to reabsorb its recent spin-offs is anybody's guess, but the political purists are readying themselves to remind us once again which term to use. It is also clear that, despite the hopes of those whose colors didn't run, there is no *former Iraq*.

The decline of the political East has led to a number of names describing the post facto reality. The Soviet Studies program at the Social Science Research Council in New York is considering switching its name either to "Post-Soviet Studies" or "Eurasian Studies." At the American University we now find "Slavic and Related Studies," while Harvard's Soviet Union program has adopted a wait-and-see attitude and will hold on to its name for now. And those inside agitators who helped bring down the Soviet beast and who used to be addressed reverentially in the Western press as "Soviet dissident so-and-so-avich" have now acquired the honorary title of "former dissident," as if the dissolution of Soviet semantics has produced unanimity in that part of the world where fighting continues and for which we await the definitive new name.

In yet more fallout from the former USSR, we are told to call the present the "post–Cold War" era, and we mark with little nostalgia the dissolution not only of the (former) East German Stasi and the (former) Soviet KGB, but also of the American SAC, the Strategic Air Command, whose continual airborne vigilance brought us *Dr. Strangelove*. While the former Soviet Union's missiles are still aimed at Western targets, and we don't know for sure whose finger is on the trigger, we're also told that we now live in a "post-nuclear" world. What's important here is remembering how to pronounce *nuclear*.

The uncertain world economy influenced our words in 1991 as well. With joblessness on the increase and layoffs all around us, employers began to *downsize* and, even more euphemistically, to *rightsize*, a word that gives the impression that our economic miseries were both necessary and proper corrections to the excesses of the past. We're firing everybody because we have come to practice the economic morality of oatmeal: it's the right thing to do. Employment counsellors, responding to this new wave, have become *outplacement experts*. Even the structure of the American family is affected: with job prospects, excuse me, I mean postemployment opportunities, being what they are, we have seen the rise of the *post-empty nest family*, one where the formerly employed former children, who have been rightsized out of their jobs, move back in with their parents to form a new nuclear family.

Perhaps the Cold War is over after all. Another word that promises to be going dormant, if not out of existence altogether, is *hostage*. For now it too has been replaced by *former hostage*. Indeed, some people are so optimistic about improvements in the post-hostage-taking political climate in the Middle East that the American University of Beirut is once again advertising teaching positions: in the 18 December, 1991, *Chronicle of Higher Education*, it ran an ad for some thirteen openings in everything from eighteenth-century English literature to Comparative Vertebrate Anatomy. There's a position in financial intermediation, which I suppose is the academic term for trading arms for hostages through the intermediary of the BCCI. There's even an opening for a social psychologist to teach conflict management and persuasion, a subject apparently still in demand in still war-torn Beirut.

All candidates for positions at the American University of Beirut are expected to hold a completed doctorate and to conduct appropriate research along with their teaching. The language of instruction is English. The AUB, as it is affectionately called, is an Affirmative-

Action, Equal-Opportunity Employer. Or is it? The ad concludes with the following pessimistic disclaimer: "U.S. passports are presently invalid for travel to, in or through Lebanon, and for residence in Lebanon, by order of the Department of State, and therefore applications from individuals who would travel to or reside in Lebanon on a U.S. passport cannot at this time be considered." (Nor is anything said of how Jewish or Israeli applicants will fare in the final selection.)

So all those rightsized American Ph.D.s looking desperately for work need not apply to what might more accurately be called the former American University of Beirut, at least until such time as a phrase like *former hostage* has proved its staying power and the nation in danger of becoming the former country of Lebanon becomes a stable political entity once again.

New Words for 1992

Let's look back at a survey of the new words that filled our lives with joy and pain in 1992, words that we used to express our deepest and our most superficial feelings. Or just some words that are fun to talk about.

Television frequently popularizes new words, so it's no surprise that some new words involve the tube. We used to look in the newspapers to find out what's on. But that means you have to read, and people watch television specifically because reading is not electronic enough for them. Now with the proliferation of cable channels and the prevalence of remote controls, sometimes called *channel flippers,* you don't have to read. You just scan the offerings by switching from channel to channel, which is called *channel surfing, trolling,* or *video grazing,* depending on whether you do it fast or slow. Too much of this will make you a *vidiot,* a word used by folks who regard TV as not intellectually correct. I suppose if you read electronic books on optical compact discs played on your TV screen, like some kind of high-brow Nintendo, you could *word-surf* the dull parts instead of skimming them.

And speaking of correct and its ilk, the formatives *-friendly, -challenged, -correct* (from *user-friendly, physically challenged,* and *politically correct*) have been productive recently, giving us *kid-friendly* as well as *earth-friendly,* and *planet-friendly,* which is one way to describe *ecotourists.* As for euphemisms, we find that *differently abled, otherly abled,* and *uniquely abled* are being used instead of *disabled,* while *challenged* has become the opposite of *abled: vertically challenged* means 'short,' and *verbally challenged* is 'illiterate' (so far, most of these are jocular terms).

Political correctness has branched out too, as *jokemeisters* become *wordmeisters* to give us *aesthetically correct, demographically correct, ecologically correct,* and *sexually correct* (don't ask me what that's supposed to mean).

Remember the old days when AT&T monopolized the telephone industry and owned all those phones, and if you were a college student with an illegal extension the telephone police would come and get you and you would never work in this town again? Well, there are so many *police* words you'd think we were living in a police state: the *sex police,* the *language police,* the *fashion police,* the *food police,* and the *science police.* There are no *police police*—not yet. With the breakup of Ma Bell, the telephone police have become decentralized, but they still have ways of making you talk.

Everybody likes to talk about the weather. The greenhouse effect, which results in global warming, is being countered by the *parasol effect,* wherein volcanic eruptions or direct hits by meteors result in huge quantities of dust and ash churned up into the air, and global cooling. Maybe the dinosaurs, creatures best described not as extinct but as *evolution-challenged,* are on their way back.

The economy has affected our vocabulary too. The down, the out, and the homeless—or should we call them the *shopping-bag-enhanced?*—practice *dumpster-diving,* which is rummaging through garbage for food or other valuables. In England, where dumps are *rubbish tips,* it's called *tip surfing. Plungers,* people who spend some time living like the homeless, or the *differently housed,* so they can write it up for the papers, practice this type of garbology as well. They spend a lot of time evading the *trash police.*

I myself learned a new word in 1992. It's *noetic,* from Greek *nous,* and means 'of or related to the mind.' It's far from brand new, but it's also far from common. I can't use it in a sentence, and probably I never will, but it has one spin-off in the new words department: what are called on the street *smart drugs,* substances reputed to improve mental performance, are called by the terminologically correct and lexicographically abled, *nootropics.*

I prefer my tropics to have sandy beaches and palm trees, especially this time of year in Central Illinois, which is *differently heated* and *oceanographically challenged,* so far as climate and geography go.

More Words in the News

One of our national newsmagazines ran a story on the proper plural of *Walkman*. Now I haven't read this story, but ignorance of the facts never stopped me before, and since the Walkman is one of the more important parts of a student's back-to-school vocabulary, here goes.

According to the latest edition of the *Random House Dictionary*—notice I didn't say Webster's, which is the generic way to refer to dictionaries—anyway, according to unabridged Random House, *Walkman* is "a brand of small portable cassette player, radio, or cassette player and radio used with headphones." They give no plural form. It is common advertising practice that trademark words are always capitalized and never inflected, but ordinary writers don't necessarily follow the guidelines of the Trademark Association, and the *Oxford English Dictionary* offers a citation referring to *Walkmans*.

Why *Walkmans*? That makes it sound like Ottomans or Mussulmans. Why not *Walkmen*? After all, the plural of *man* is *men*. Some people resist *Walkmen* because it seems a sexist term. But the plural is no more sexist than the singular, which has produced the sex-neutral parody, *Walkperson*, with its own cumbersome plural, *Walkpersons*.

But the main resistance to *Walkmen* comes from Sony itself, the originator of the device. Because they want to protect their trademark, and prevent it from becoming a generic, Sony wants us to say the very long plural, *Walkman personal stereos*.

As a trademark, *Walkman* means money in the bank for Sony. The manufacturer has a vested interest in making the brand name popular, but it can't let that name become a generic term, and this is a real danger for *Walkman*: what else are you going to call those little schmendricks you wear on your head while you jog or sit in large lecture classes? *Personal stereos* sounds more like a hygiene product—something that will make your ears feel fresher and smell better.

Lots of brand names have become generic. *Xerox* runs ads with a Charles Addams cartoon depicting a trademark graveyard: each gravestone bears the name of a trademark that became generic, including *linoleum, dry ice, raisin bran, nylon, kerosene, trampoline, cube steak, escalator, corn flakes, yo-yo,* and *shredded wheat*. That's because *Xerox*, which is already for most people a generic for photocopy, is worried.

Kimberley-Clark, the makers of *Kleenex*, another word that many of us use as a generic, prints a little booklet called "Why in the world should you care for our trademarks?"

The answer to that question is simple: if we as consumers and writers preserve Kimberley-Clark's trademarks, they will make more money. That's like saying, what's good for General Motors is good for the country. And the trademark people do have some clout: when *Webster's Third New International Dictionary* was published in 1961, it did not capitalize any head words, including trademarks (I think they may have made an exception for *God*). But pressure from the Trademark Association forced the publishers to change their practice, and in subsequent reprintings of the dictionary, many pages had to be reset to capitalize terms that were wholly owned by private enterprise.

The makers of Kleenex tell us to follow two simple rules when using trademarks: treat a trademark with distinction, which means use boldface type or at least capitalize it when you write it, and treat a trademark as an adjective, and adjectives don't have plurals (I think it was Shelley Berman who did a routine about the plural of *Kleenex* being *kleenices*, like the plural of *stewardess* being *stewardi*). Anyway, don't say, "Gimme a Kleenex, I gotta sneeze." Hold that sneeze until you say the proper "Please pass a Kleenex brand facial tissue, because I am in sudden need of superior nasal protection."

So the next time you're in class or out on the jogging trail and you have a desperate urge to listen to your local national public radio affiliate, remember to say, "Please pass the *Walkman personal stereo*."

Dial 1-800-M4MURDR

Did you ever see those ads where if you want to order you're supposed to call up a phone number that isn't a number but a series of letters? You know, they say things like, "To order just dial 1-800-ITSAGYP."

These aren't phone numbers, they're phone words. The phone company calls them vanity phone numbers, like the vanity license plates (10SNE1) and the vanity call letters of some radio and TV stations—remember WKRP and WIOU? And they are definitely on the increase.

For years a Chicago rug store advertised its phone number as C-A-R-P-E-T-S, but it was virtually alone in the phone-word game. Now, vanity phone numbers are everywhere. In an hour of looking through magazines, I managed to collect the following: if you want someone to sell an invention for you, call 1-800-288-IDEA. Allied Van Lines' number is 1-800-367-MOVE. Need to incorporate in Delaware for tax purposes? Just dial 1-800-321-CORP. How about something from Giorgio of Beverly Hills? Try 1-800-GIORGIO. Not so upscale?

Then call Mary Kay cosmetics at 1-800-MARY KAY. If you want a car, there's 1-800-GO-TOYOTA. Or try 1-800-4ABUICK and 1-800-4ACHRYSLER. For a Florida vacation, 1-407-WDISNEY. Going south of the border? Dial 1-800-44-MEXICO. If you want to get fancier, try 1-800-CLUB MED. To invest in America's future there's 1-800-US BONDS. To open a Citibank account, 1-800-321-CITI. And to save the whales, you can reach the World Wildlife Fund at 1-800-CALL-WWF. Subscribing to *Ladybug*, a magazine for children? Call 1-800-BUG PALS. Speaking of kids, if you have a question about a toy you can call 1-800-PLAYSKL, a phone word so valuable to its owner that Playskool has registered it as a trademark (I'm not sure why they've bothered, since I can't imagine infringing on a phone number).

Continuing the list of phone words, for a free hearing test, there's 1-800-EARS, and for contacts, 1-800-432-LENS. You can learn about Nikon sunglasses at 1-800-NIKON US. And you can get a watch by dialing 1-800-CARTIER. On Fridays a tiny ad at the bottom of page one of the *New York Times* advises Jewish women and girls to call 1-800-SABBATH to find out what time to light Shabbat candles (if there's no answer, you know you've called too late). And a Chicago billboard announces that the Virgin Mary speaks to America twenty-four hours a day at 1-800-882-MARY. Not Jewish or Catholic? Not to worry: if you're lonely and New Age, you can reach an astrological matchmaker at 1-800-MATCH-ME.

Educational institutions are switching to phone words in a big way. To reach New York University, just dial 1-800-262-4NYU. New York's fashion Institute of Technology sports 1-800-GO-TO-FIT. Mercy College is at 1-800-MERCY NY. The Academy for Culinary Arts cooked up the number 1-800-645-CHEF. And Audrey Cohen College offers a variety of degree programs at 1-800-33-THINK. If you're not ready for college yet, Stanley H. Kaplan can help at 1-800-KAP-TEST. And you can even get a tape to teach you to read by calling 1-800-ABCDEFG, but of course you have to know part of the alphabet to be able to do that.

Twenty years ago, when phone spelling was in its infancy, I had some friends who lived in a Massachusetts commune. They were only too delighted to find that their phone number spelled A-L-I-V-I-N-G. Prompted by their enthusiasm, I tried to translate my own phone number into words, but the best I could get was R-A-W-G-O-O-K—unpleasant, if not downright insulting. My formerly communal friends all live in suburbs and work for IBM today. I'm still here at the typewriter (all right, it *is* a word processor), still spelling phone numbers.

The possibilities of finding appropriate phone words to match telephone subscribers are almost endless (actually, imagining appropriate phone words is more interesting than collecting the ones businesses choose for themselves). I suppose the *New Yorker* magazine's number is 212-BIG-SNOB. If you want the Girl Scouts try dialing COOKIES. Posing as a doctor? For a fast diploma, there's 1-800-QUACK MD. You can get a cheap lawyer at 217-CHASERS and a discount broker by dialing 555-SCAM. Want to remake a classic film? Dial 1-800-M4MURDR.

Of course there are limitations on phone words. For one thing, American phone numbers are seven digits long, and so we are limited to the set of words or combinations of words containing no more than seven letters. And not everyone can have a phone word. The numbers 1 and 0 have no letters attached, so if your number has a 1 or a 0 it won't spell a thing. In addition, a phone word should contain at least one vowel. And not all of the alphabet is available on your telephone, either. For some odd reason there's no *Q* and no *Z* on the dial, so a testing center can't have a phone word like ZIPQUIZ and you can't reach the community mental health project by dialing GO CRAZY, though you could try 1-800-HUNG-UP.

I suppose everyone's using phone words now because they think it's easier to remember a word than a string of numbers. That's certainly true for a number like 222-TAXI. But even if phone words are memorable, they're not particularly easy to use. When you go to dial one you have to translate the letters back into numbers, which takes a bit of work, because each button on the phone has one large number with three tiny letters squeezed above it so you have to squint real hard, especially if you don't have your reading glasses on.

And these phone words are certainly not spelled for your convenience—let's suppose you run a charity and your number is RECEIVE. How many people have to stop and think whether it's *i-e* or *e-i* after *c*? And what about the exceptions to that rule? The phone company gives you credit if you misdial a number. But just like those old no-crossing-out spelling tests in school, with phone words everything changes: you don't get your quarter back if you misspell the word you're dialing.

How easy are these phone words to remember, anyway, especially since most of them involve dialing a combination of words and numbers, like 1-717-22SPEND or 312-5RIPOFF? I wonder if there's a phonewords *Yellow Pages* yet, or would it have to be called a *phone dictionary*? To find out if my fingers could do the walking, I tried calling ATT-SPEL. It was busy, but I imagine that when the operator finally does answer, he or she says, "Word, please."

Maybe the increasing popularity of phone words signals a resistance to the fact that our lives are being defined by numbers more and more. Or they may be just a throwback to the old days when every phone number began with a real word, called an exchange. I fondly recall phone numbers beginning Ironsides, Stillwell, Ravenswood, and University. And speaking of *Dial M*, don't forget the film that catapulted Elizabeth Taylor to (adult) stardom, *Butterfield 8*. Surely there's something about a word that gives you more identity. I suppose that's why people have names instead of serial numbers.

By the way, since there are three letters for every number on the dial, you always risk being sandbagged by synonyms. A single phone number can have several spellings. A rug store can be CARPETS and a kennel can be BASSETS, but not if they're in the same area code, because both enumerate as 227-7387.

All the vanity phone numbers I've found so far are assigned to businesses, but according to the phone company there's nothing to prevent individuals from getting phone numbers that spell a word. So if you're interested in getting your own vanity phone number, consult the front matter of your local phone book for details (for example, Illinois Bell currently charges a one-time fee of $38 for such custom-number service). And if you want to call me with your comments, you can reach me at FDE-BFXC. That's also spelled EED-CFYA. Out of town, call A1S-DFF-AEWB. Operators are standing by, so don't forget, call before midnight tonight.

The Tough Get Going

It was either Ehrlichman or Haldemann, the Rosencrantz and Guildenstern of the Nixon administration, or one of the other honchos of the Watergate era, who said, perhaps not for the first time, "When the going gets tough, the tough get going." Who are *the tough*? If today's use of the word is any indication, I suppose the tough are truly getting soft.

Maybe I'm being hopelessly sentimental, but I remember a time when *tough* was a pretty tough word. Or at least a strong one. Being *tough* was the opposite of being civilized or cultured. *Tough guys* were to be avoided, and secretly emulated. *Tough* was gangster pictures:

Cagney was tough, and Bogie, and Eddie Robinson, and Lauren Bacall. It was the hat worn slanted on the side of your head, the cigarette dangling from the mouth. Of course the real gangsters were no pussycats compared to the actors who portrayed them. How else could they dangle cigarettes from their mouths and not blink when the smoke got in their eyes? Even Hemingway's toughness was not suspect: We didn't ask then, the way we do now, "What defect in his masculinity was he overcompensating for?"

But *tough* has always meant positive things as well—being resolute in dealing with the opposition, strict or inflexible in the legal sense, capable of great physical endurance, aggressive. A *tough nut to crack* is still a difficult problem to solve, or a difficult person to figure out or manipulate. The verb *to tough it out*, an American slang expression dating from the 1830s, meaning 'to withstand difficult conditions to the end, without flinching,' is still applied when the going gets tough.

So what has happened to take the starch out of *tough*? Nowadays, *tough* has become the darling of the media and public relations set. We used to think of iron as tough; now it's plastic garbage bags that get the designation. We are told that guys who are overweight and short of breath and can't punch their way out of Hefty bags are *tough* administrators making *tough* decisions—like cutting back on paper-clip consumption or turning widows and orphans out of apartments they are converting into condominiums.

Politicians who can't remember their own names, who have their every word scripted and researched in advance by masseuses and spin doctors, talk *tough* to the Reds at photo opportunities with visiting 4-H delegations. And judges are *tough* when they hand down suspended sentences to *tougher* patriots from the career military who have spent their lives behind desks shuffling the papers they are about to shred. It used to be junkyard dogs who were *tough*, now its junk-bond dealers who have never lifted anything heavier than a leveraged buy out.

Surveying newspapers over the past five years—don't worry, I didn't read all of them, I searched them with a tough new computer data base—we see that *tough* is applied to London stockbrokers as well as Mexican strongmen, to designing the modern office as well as forcing unproductive workers into retirement, to computer sales as well as to predicting Congressional votes. And of course to *love*. *Tough love* means hurting the ones you love because you love them. Of course, Oscar Wilde had the idea long before it hit American pop psychology, but at least Wilde, who one would never have called tough despite the fact he had to endure some pretty incredible hardship, didn't think you hurt the ones you love for their own good.

Will all this tough talk weaken *tough*? Probably not. Language is tough, and *tough* will be here when we're all gone.

The Word Zoo

Although *the dictionary* has become a generic expression to mean 'a source of meanings or spellings,' there are actually many dictionaries, and many words for dictionary. Dictionary, thesaurus, chrestomathy, lexicon, vocabulary, word hoard: these are our words for collections of words. Why do we have so many words for word lists? Not because we like the job of assembling them. Samuel Johnson, who spent twenty years of his life writing a dictionary in order to make money, defined the lexicographer as 'a harmless drudge.' Some people use *Webster's* as a generic name for dictionary, but no dictionary records this interesting fact. And although people like to use the phrase "the dictionary says" quite a bit, dictionaries are certainly not popular because people like to read them cover to cover, or even a page at a time. In fact, while almost every college-educated person owns some sort of dictionary, which they probably got as a high-school graduation present from a not particularly doting relative, most people's dictionaries lie idle most of the time.

The dictionary market is a big one, and highly competitive, but surprisingly enough, while dictionary marketers put a lot of effort into determining what moves their books off store shelves, I don't think they look very closely at how people use their dictionaries. Publishers boast proudly of the greater numbers of words in each new edition. *The Random House College Dictionary* claims "more than 170,000 entries, many more than any comparable dictionary," and its successor, *The Random House Webster's College Dictionary*, ups that by another 10k. And all the dictionaries automatically raise the count a couple of hundred words by defining the numbers one to one hundred. For example the Random House tells us that *twenty* is "a cardinal number, 10 times 2." *Twentieth*, which of course comes before *twenty* alphabetically, is defined as "next after the nineteenth; being the ordinal number for twenty." Somehow I knew that.

The Random House College Dictionary offers a list of U.S. and Canadian colleges. How many times do you need to look up Mt. Aloysius Jr. College in Cresson PA, ZIP code 16630, a small, fully-accredited private school founded in 1939 which offers an associate degree in nursing? In the back, too, there is a list of given names which tells you, for example, that *Rachel* is Hebrew for 'lamb' (actually, it means 'lamb of God,' which is something just a wee bit different in connotation).

I'll tell you what I used dictionaries for before I became a professional language person. When I was young I stared for hours at the double-page spread of the flags of all the countries, which was followed by the pages depicting military medals and insignia. I admit to browsing through the text as well, looking for interesting words—OK, I tried to look up the dirty words, but in those days dictionaries didn't have the four letter ones, and they defined the longer ones in Latin, which didn't do me any good at all.

It seems to me that the dictionary is the word-equivalent of a zoo, a controlled environment where we isolate words from their natural habitat, so that we can look them over one at a time, not jumbled together into sentences. Safe in their dictionary cage they can't bite us, not the way they can in books. In the word zoo we can see how cute words like *leptokurtic* and *lucubrate* really are. Actually I'm lucubrating right now, but if you want to know what that means, and whether or not it's a suitable thing to do in public, you'll have to take a trip to your local dictionary. It's open year round and there are very few regulations. The sign in front says No Running, No Skateboards, No Loud Music, and Please Don't Feed the Words.

A Zoo by Any Other Name

Speaking of zoos, there was in the Spring of 1993 an attempt to rename one of the world's most famous zoos. Will the Bronx Zoo go the way of Sixth Avenue? Not if the Bronx members of the New York City Council can help it. For them, the Zoo will always be a zoo, and they oppose the decision of the New York Zoological Society to rename the Bronx Zoo, and all the other zoos under its management, "Wildlife Conservation Parks." That's a name that has even less pizzazz than "Avenue of the Americas," which has been the official name of Sixth Avenue for forty years or more, though almost nobody uses it.

A zoo has been a place where you go to gawk at the animals, and where they collect to gawk back at you, since 1847, when the shortened form of *zoological garden* first appears in the word-zoo that is the dictionary. But the recent name change suggests that the word *zoo* may itself be an endangered species.

Is *zoo* no longer an appropriate name for a collection of animals? Words, once launched, develop new meanings that often conflict with their original sense. Sometimes, too, the original sense becomes tainted by the new one: so *rhetoric* once meant 'convincing speech,' and now it means 'hot air.' Today it is almost impossible to divorce rhetoric from hot air. The conflict between the zookeepers and the city government—it is not clear which group has ultimate jurisdiction over which zoo—is a perfect example of this.

Like *rhetoric, zoo* has developed a transferred sense, one which bothers the New York Zoological Society. For the last sixty years or so *zoos* have meant not only collections of fauna but also assemblies of not-always-enviable people. Oxford was described as a zoo of dons in 1935. This sense is mildly derogatory, and the newest sense of *zoo*, "a place marked by rampant confusion, disorder," or "unrestrained behavior," which is even more negative, has prompted the New York zookeepers to make the switch. If you say "The trading pit at the Commodities Exchange is a real zoo," you are diminishing the image of the real zoo, or so the Zoological Society fears.

Up to now, wildlife conservation parks have evoked images of Kenya, or maybe the Florida Everglades: someplace inaccessible to everything except 600-meter telephoto lenses where people are doing their best to preserve nature in the wild and keep endangered species from going extinct. Now they are to include the darkest Bronx as well. Calling a zoo a zoo no longer appeals to zookeepers, who fear that the public will think real zoos have become places of confusion, disorder, and unrestrained behavior.

Even if you think the real wildlife of the Bronx is outside the zoo and consists mainly of pigeons, rats, roaches, a few garage bands, and the occasional victim of an early-release mental health program, you might wonder why anyone should want to replace the succinct, it-says-it-all word, *zoo*, with a mouthful of rhetorical fluff. The Zoological Society runs the risk of turning wildlife conservation into a rhetorical abstraction. Zoos, even the great one in the Bronx, have too much concrete to pass themselves off as the Serengeti Plain, even to a city kid like me.

What else is on the hit list of those afraid to call a zoo a zoo? If consistency is virtuous, then the Children's Zoo must be relabeled the Children's Wildlife Conservation Park, which will only make the children want to stay home and play Nintendo even more than they already do. And while they're at it, why not rechristen the Botanical Gardens? Unlike the zoo, the Bronx Botanical Gardens never got a snappy name. "The bo" would be the logical abbreviation. *Botanical garden* hasn't developed a negative connotation like *zoo*, but why wait until that happens? Surely the time is not far off when it will become the term of choice for 'a piece of land full of broken glass, beer cans, and old refrigerators, defined along at least two sides of its perimeter by abandoned cars,' and some wag will quip, "That vacant lot near the school has sure become a botanical garden—it's a regular bo— since the city took it over." So while we're at it, let's change *botanical garden* to something like *Hyperallergenic Flora Propagation and Preservation Observation Facility* before the name is lost to us forever as a place to go to sniff the flowers.

10 Last Words

Old words don't only go into spelling bees when they die. They go into old dictionaries and libraries. But with overcrowding and underfunding, there is a move afoot to kick our homeless words out of their refuge and place them back on the street, where they will be made to fend for themselves, to the discomfort and embarrassment of the rest of the vocabulary. Recently I received in the mail a list of Middle English words that a dictionary maker wants to bring back. Middle English—used roughly from the twelfth to the fifteenth century—was a period of great linguistic variety and growth, but many of its words have not survived. For example, there's *soupet,* a small portion of broth or soup. Not a common word in Middle English, when the marketing concept of soup-for-one had not yet developed. (For that matter, the concept of marketing concept hadn't even developed.) *Soupet* appears only once in the written record of Middle English. But think what a boon it would be to today's soup-sellers if instead of offering their single servings, which emphasize the consumer's miserable, eat-alone existence, they could sell *soupets* of bouillabaisse or chicken with stars? For the extra-hungry lone consumer you could even have *super soupets.*

We've lost more words in English than you can spell with an alphabet soupet. Some of them have left traces: there's *kempt,* which meant 'combed,' and lives on in *unkempt,* and *gust,* whose trace we find in *disgust.* Word gamesters love to recover such lost positives and make long lists of them in case they ever play Scrabble with a historian of the language.

One lost word we might bring back, according to our Middle English lexicographer, is *forshuppild,* 'changed for the worse.' It's a forceful, expressive statement without being distasteful: *This soupet is forshuppild* is so much nicer than *This soup is disgusting.* If you like the soup, say it is *gusty.* On the other hand, if you still want to complain, you could use another fine old dead word, *grutchen*—it means 'to complain, or grouch.'

Reviving old words may not be as profitable as inventing new ones. The *Wall Street Journal* reports a couple of firms who devise and sell new words to their business clients, but I've never seen a Used Word Shop—or one where the stock is not used but "prespoken." I doubt that such businesses stay open very long. But seriously friends, why not try an old word today. Old words may not save you time and money, but they do make English more *facundious*—that's an old word for eloquent or elegant of speech.

The Power of Words

Physicists speak of the great forces of nature: gravity, electromagnetism, and the stuff that holds atoms together. But language also draws us together and splits us apart with a violence we can measure in megatons.

The evidence of the power of language is all around us. Formulas like the Pledge of Allegiance become political magic as we either wrap the flag around our tongues, or make a political statement by not making a statement at pledge time. Individual words become taboo. Actors call *Macbeth* "The Scottish Play" because they fear its real name brings bad luck. And words like *liberal* or *recession* or *cancer* are so dangerous we often refer to them by their initial letters: the *l*-word, the *r*-word, the *c*-word.

Language is so important to us that we require students in school to study English, a language most of them already speak. Sometimes we even make them study a foreign language, though at other times we try to suppress those languages. During World War I, many American schools banned the teaching of German, and some states forbade the use of any language other than English in public.

Language seems most powerful when it is bound up in books. Books entertain and teach us. But books also insult or threaten us, and this is when we react to their words most harshly. We find books that are unkind to Catholics, Protestants, Jews, Muslims, Atheists, Blacks, Women, Men, children, Europeans, Asians, the middle class, the poor, the rich, the government, the family, space invaders, teachers, the mentally ill, psychologists, and even radio language commentators, among others. When it comes to books, nothing and everything is sacred.

When people feel attacked by books, they often try to suppress them. The flap over Muslim author Salman Rushdie's novel *The Satanic Verses* is just one in a long series of reactions demonstrating the extreme power of words and the need people feel to attack or defend the word.

Writing has always been a dangerous profession. Chaucer, Boccaccio, and Galileo acceded to pressure to disown their words. Darwin's *Origin of Species*, published more than 100 years ago, still sparks book burnings and lawsuits. *The Merchant of Venice* and *Huckleberry Finn* are regularly swept from library shelves in the United States. James Joyce's *Ulysses* and D. H. Lawrence's *Lady Chatterly's Lover,* now considered landmarks in the history of the novel, were initially banned in this country for their sexual explicitness. Even *The American Heritage Dictionary*—which is, after all, a collection of the most powerful words in the language arranged alphabetically for our convenience—has been banned by some of our school districts.

I went to school when J. D. Salinger's *Catcher in the Rye* was forbidden because its hero, a teenager named Holden Caulfield, used "bad language." Of course I read it as soon as I could get my hands on it. Later I taught in a high school where Philip Roth's novel *Portnoy's Complaint* was kept in the library—but only teachers were allowed to read it. The school was protecting students from the very words they were spray-painting all over the schoolyard.

The Last Temptation of Christ, the novel by Nikos Kazantzakis, who is better known in this country for his *Zorba the Greek,* was a relatively minor literary work before it became a movie attacked by mobs of fundamentalists who hadn't seen it, but who felt insulted by it nonetheless. Similarly, more people object to "The Islamic Novel" than can have waded through its obscure prose.

I suppose the ultimate demonstration of the force of words in the universe is the fact that people burn books and attack writers without reading them first. True, this saves time, but it also shows how words can become so threatening we just close our eyes and ears to them. Is it really the words themselves that do harm, or our fear that gives them power to control us? I know what Holden Caulfield would say about that, and it's not "sticks and stones can break my bones."

What's Wrong with This Sentence?

I was observing an English class last year, and the teacher put a sentence on the board, which is just the kind of thing English teachers do. The sentence was, "The Thrift Shop is giving free gifts to the children of the poor." The teacher then intoned that traditional English-teacher line, "What's wrong with this sentence?"

That's just the kind of question I get asked all the time.

Well, "What's wrong" wasn't obvious to the students, who shifted about uncomfortably in their seats until one of them suggested that *children of the poor* was wordy, and wouldn't it be better to say *poor children?*

"What about 'free gifts'?" asked the instructor hopefully, and after another bit of shuffling a student hesitantly offered the opinion that all gifts were free.

"Yes!" the instructor pounced, relieved that at least one student had connected. The logic here is faultless. Indeed, the expression *free gift* has been scorned by usage critics for twenty years, so our English teacher is in good company. The argument goes that, since all gifts are free, *free gifts* is redundant, repetitive, tautological. It says the same thing twice. So it's wrong. Right? Well, now, let's not rush to conclusions. After all, English is full of expressions which seem at first to defy logic. Let's start by examining some other expressions which show similar problems.

How about *natural popcorn?* The vending machine near my office sells, along with chips and candy, something they call *natural popcorn.* What's wrong with that phrase? Well, what other kind of popcorn is there except natural popcorn? I mean, OK, so the stuff that comes out of the bag is exploded from hard little kernels of corn, which my *Random House College Dictionary* tells us is a tall, annual cereal plant, *Zea Mays.* It may be a little stale, but hey, it is natural. It is not made from Styrofoam—though it tastes like it is. So much for natural popcorn.

Here's another one: *in-depth summary.* A local radio station advertises in one of its self-promotions that it provides the listener with in-depth summaries of the news every morning. Now, my *Random House College Dictionary* kindly informs me that *summaries* are concise, brief digests. They are anything but deep, certainly not *in-depth.* There is a clear distinction to be made between a summary of the news and the news itself, or so the words seem to imply. So what is an in-depth summary? It sounds like there ain't no such animal.

Are all these expressions wrong, then? Can we righteously condemn in-depth summaries and natural popcorn and free gifts? Certainly the temptation is there, but perhaps we go too far when we force language into a logical mold, in these particular cases, anyway.

Before we rush to judgment, let's look at what the audience, the reader, the listener, expects from these phrases. For example, we don't expect the radio or television news to present detailed stories— for that we go to print. We expect summaries from radio. What this particular *public* radio station is emphasizing is that its news is more detailed than most, and it is not reduced to sound bites sandwiched between high-decibel commercial breaks. Similarly, *natural popcorn* attempts to defeat our expectation that vending machine food is not only stale, it is also composed in large part of nonbiodegradable materials (*chemicals,* if you will).

And *free gift,* like the nonexistent free lunch, is nature's way of reminding us that we have come to suspect that every gift has strings attached. It's an expression that says, "Hey, this one really is free. No salesperson will call. There is no obligation to buy. Honest."

If you look at it that way, then there is nothing wrong with these expressions. Of course that doesn't mean we believe them. I don't send for free gifts or eat natural popcorn that tastes like Styrofoam. But I do bring you in-depth summaries of the English language in these essays. Two out of three's not bad.

A Preferred Customer

Don't get me wrong, I do have my gripes and quibbles with language, just like everybody else. Here is one of them. Merchants are using a new classification in an attempt to flatter us into spending more of our money. We used to be patrons, shoppers, consumers, or the public. Now we're all of us "preferred customers." When I stopped at a stationery store on my lunch hour to buy some large envelopes, the clerk asked me if I had a preferred-customer card. "What is that?" I wanted to know, though I already suspected what the answer would be. A preferred-customer card is available to anyone who asks for one, she explained, and all you have to do to be a preferred customer is have a preferred-customer card. But the card carries no perks. With it, plus some cash, a local one-party check numbered over 500, or an approved credit card, you will get your envelopes. Then I got an advertisement in the mail from a drugstore chain addressed not with my name but with the words "A Preferred Customer." But I wasn't fooled by my new title. I knew that for this merchant, preferred customer is just another way of saying "occupant."

In reality, then, a preferred customer is not someone on a first-name basis with the boss, not a frequent shopper or a big spender, or even someone who actually buys something, since the term can apply to anyone who just comes in to browse. In the extreme case of the pharmacy a preferred customer is anyone on the mailing list, anyone with a legitimate address, anyone, that is, who isn't homeless.

Of course there are still situations where *preferred* has some meaning. On Wall Street, preferred stock beats common stock to dividends, and in the event of bankruptcy, to company assets, if there are any left. And on the international scene, preferred trading status means giving better deals to preferred customers, the discounts that apply within the British Commonwealth or the European Community. Globally speaking, preferred customers are what the American government calls "most favored nations," and they are a group from which some countries are excluded.

But in the domestic American marketplace, where money talks and nobody walks, where we are all equally capitalist regardless of accidents of birth, preference is freely distributed to all who have the ability to pay. I'm tempted to claim that the term derives from the fact that merchants prefer customers, and they use the designation to try to persuade customers that they are special. Under capitalism, all customers may be equal, goes the Orwellian message, but some are more equal than others. But I'm not persuaded by this feeble attempt at stroking. Instead, I am convinced that *preferred* in this sense has lost just about all of its meaning. Calling me a preferred customer simply because I have cold cash or credit, or a mail drop, doesn't seem like much of a compliment.

Preference literally means 'putting something before, advancing it to the head of the line.' A preference can be special treatment, a promotion, an advantage. Herman Melville wrote a story called "Bartleby, the Scrivener," in which the protagonist, Bartleby, who is an office worker, responds to his employer's requests by saying "I would prefer not to." There is an irony, and a certain sadness, in Bartleby's constant refusal to engage with life. But there is a vitality in the use of *prefer* that I don't see when I am invited to become a preferred customer.

It's not that I think commercialism is fatal to language. Quite the opposite: I'm convinced that, on balance, the business world uses language creatively—it takes chances with words that our most radical literary artists are reluctant to take, and it influences the direction of English by keeping it always in our consciousness. I just think in this case it falls kind of flat. So from now on, when I'm asked to become a preferred customer, I'll just answer, "I would prefer not to."

Do You Like Music?

A reporter once asked me if I liked music. How it bears on language you will see in a moment. My answer, of course, was "Yes." But I thought to myself, "Who would say no to such an apple pie question?"

Of course I like music. As an amateur, which means someone who *likes* rather than someone who *does*. Little did I know we weren't talking about the same word.

Now, I am not as amateurish as some of my friends, who spout the latest sound technology, talk music with the conviction of digitized liner notes, and know intimate details of the lives of the composers and artists, which they rehearse ad nauseam. But I like music. Or rather, some music. Not the music my reporter meant, though.

He proceeded to toss out the names of some groups he was intimate with. I don't remember them, but they sounded like the kinds of groups you hear of nowadays—Citizen's Arrest, Nuclear Winter, Dog's Breakfast.

Slowly I came to the realization that the reporter really meant did I like rock music, or popular music, or whatever the appropriate classification is for the output of Dead Cat on a Line, Insider Trading, or the Superconducting Supercolliders.

It's a question of semantics. (Usually when someone says that, they mean that semantics isn't important. Of course when I say it as a language commentator I mean it literally: semantics *means* 'meanings.') And here's where language comes in. When a general term becomes more specific in its meaning, we call this process narrowing. *Meat* once meant food of any kind. As in *nutmeat*. Now it means animal flesh. Similarly deer once meant an animal; now it refers to one particular kind of animal, like Bambi. That's narrowing.

So *music*, which once meant 'music,' now at least to some people seemsto mean only the stuff played by the Red Brigade, Worker Ants, or the Lotus Eaters. I can live with changes in meaning. You could say that as a historian of the English language I couldn't live without them. But I have to admit to feeling some discomfort with the notion that what I think of as music is excluded categorically by lots of people.

Maybe I shouldn't be surprised. People who are serious about their music *are* exclusive: they won't stand for what is old-fashioned, or newfangled, or derivative, or in an elevator. The Society for Ancient Computer Music rejects anything not played on original instruments, by which they probably mean Univacs with tubes instead of transistors and microchips, or maybe even old acoustic Burroughs adding machines in the percussion section.

Maybe the kind of music I like would be more commercially viable if the groups who played it picked more trendy names. Like the Deaf Beethoven String Quartet or The Houston Chainsaw Symphony Orchestra. Then if someone asks, "Do you like music?" we might be on closer wavelengths.

I suppose it was only a matter of time—and here at last is the tie-in with language teaching—but now there's a rock group who call themselves *Bad English*. Aha, I say to myself, this should be music to my ears, by which I mean not literal music but the stuff of language commentary (and that's semantic widening, the opposite of narrowing). I don't suppose I'd care very much for the actual music Bad English plays. (Maybe I wouldn't even call it music.) What would my colleagues say? But I don't think that, even though I'm an English teacher, I would like a group called "Good English" any better. I mean, they'd probably sing things like that old soul hit, "I Do Not Get Any Satisfaction." Or Gershwin's "It Is Not Necessarily So." Or they might reprise the repertory of that mainstream rock group, The *Whom*.

Read My Shirt

If you're worried about the so-called literacy crisis; if you think that video and film have replaced the verbal image with the visual; if you believe that progressive education and permissive discipline have created us a nation of non-readers; if you are willing to bet, as we slouch toward the end of the twentieth century, that the death of the word is at hand; my friends, if you're as down about literacy in America as all that, well then, you can just read my shirt.

That's right. America's clothing manufacturers have come to the rescue. They've solved our most pressing educational problem, the decline in reading ability, with the newest fashion phenomenon, WORDS ON SHIRTS, little or no ironing required. If you doubt me, do what I did one night: go to your nearest department store and look at the racks. Forget about whole language versus phonics. Shirts will soon replace flashcards as the high road to reading. You'll get back to basics with the new skill clothing.

Now we've all seen printed clothing: one of the most common is the college sweatshirt. They even sell sweatshirts for schools where students don't wear sweatshirts, like Oxford or the Sorbonne. And of course there are the message T-shirts, telling us to save the whales, or the ozone layer, or fatalistically reminding us that some four-letter words happen.

But clothing has gone beyond all that. Now there are shirts that tell you absolutely nothing at all, in big letters, for example, INTERNATIONAL NEWS or HIBERNATION INSTITUTE, the latter followed by the mock-Latin slogan, SLEEPUS AD INFINITUM. I see shirts that say PRIMITIVE CLUB and MADE IN U.S.A. (I checked the label; they are).

These are nonsense shirts, random collections of words like the one which reads REGULATION PEDESTRIAN DESTINATION INSPECTION SPEED LIMIT 75, which I suppose is just a vocabulary list for a driver's license test. But there are shirts as well with little stories on them, like "I like to give hearts to my best friend. She gives me hearts too. Sometimes we give someone new a heart so they will know that we think they are nice." I even saw a shirt that went all the way, pretending to be not just a page but an entire book: it said VOLUME 6, SERIES FOUR, SPORTS AND LEISURE.

It's only a hop and a skip from flashcard clothing to literary wear for more advanced readers. This could be the best marketing ploy since Classic Comics. Here's the scenario. It's late at night, you can't sleep, you go out to menswear or young juniors for something to read. Here's Homer's *Odyssey* in prose translation on an overall (or a condensed version on a shortall); Dickens' *A Tale of Two Cities* on two shirts, Paris and London, for the layered look ("It was the best of clothes, it was the worst of clothes"). There's Swift's *Tale of a Tub*, hand-wash warm, dry flat, or Milton's *Paradise Lost* in 100% cotton, use no bleach. If you don't fancy ironing, how about James Joyce's *Ulysses* in polyester, or the Book of Job in stone-washed 14 oz. denim?

Shirt reading is about to become the hottest thing since personal stereos. Freshmen won't write papers, they'll write clothing. Parents will yell, "I thought I told you to hang up your books." And standardized tests will bow to the new trend: "Do not open this shirt until the proctor tells you to. You are not expected to finish this shirt. You may only write on this shirt using a number 2 pencil. Hey you, over there—yes, you—eyes on your own shirt."

Daddy Eats Bushes

A lot of parents feel they have to police their children's grammar. Not only is it a thankless task, they're probably wasting their time if they try. I don't mean that children shouldn't speak correctly. Of course they should. Whatever "correctly" means. But it seems that the more adults try to get them to do things, the less children seem to produce the appropriate response. You can sweet-talk them, cajole them, revile them, punish them, bribe them, and send them to their rooms. But they still talk like kids. Pediatricians routinely assure parents that all normal children will dress themselves and wash their own hair without crying and give up bottles and diapers by the time they're twenty-one, and probably a good deal earlier, so why worry? They may even clean up their own rooms. And somewhere along the line they'll start sounding like adults, and you'll start missing all those "darndest things" that Art Linkletter used to bribe children on his radio and TV shows to say.

Of course I have an example or two of cute kid sayings saved up. Here's one.

The waitress set the salads down as we prepared to embark on the ill-advised adventure called "Dining Out with Kids." (Actually she wasn't a waitress but a server, but if I say, "The server set the salads down," you probably wouldn't know what I was talking about, and there'd be too many words starting with *s*.)

Anyway, my son was two at the time. He had finished destroying the kids' menu and was casting about for new ways to depopulate the restaurant, when he looked over at the pale green bits of vegetation on my little plate, spiced with what the restaurants insist on calling not just pepper but "fresh ground pepper," and asked with the seriousness of one who has just made a discovery of universal proportions, "Daddy eat bushes?" Before I could explain about edible and inedible vegetation and how only grown-ups knew what green things you could and couldn't put in your mouth, he climbed up the back seat of the booth and began staring intently at a man who had clearly never dismembered a crab before and surely didn't need a juvenile kibbitzer to help him.

Children have a way of giving words the surprising pungency that "fresh ground pepper" lacks. After we told Jonathan several times that he needed a fresh diaper, he concluded that *fresh* meant 'new' and extended the word to all sorts of new situations: if he's finished with a toy he asks for a *fresh* one, and if he's angry when his parents tell him not to eat the neighbor's bushes he demands *fresh* parents.

The linguistic creativity children display is often funny. In 1969, Amsel Greene, a high school teacher, coined a term to describe the way kids mash words and extract meaning from the resulting nonsense. A colleague showed Greene a sentence a student had written: "In 1957 Eugene O'Neill won a Pullet Surprise." *Pullet,* or 'chicken,' comes from the Latin for 'young animal,' and the Pullet Surprises Greene subsequently collected from her young students include these definitions: *stalemate,* 'a husband or wife who is no longer interesting'; *homogeneous,* 'handy man around the house'; and *deciduous,* 'able to make up one's mind quickly.' A *dilemma* is what you get when you graduate. *Parsimonious* means 'having to do with grammar.' A *tenet* is a singing group with ten people in it. A *peccadillo* is 'a bullfighter,' probably the one carrying the shovel. And *vindictive* is rather appropriately defined as 'one of the moods of grammar.'

Sometimes the definition is clarified with an exemplary sentence: "By the time the police found him, metamorphosis had set in." Sometimes etymology gives the clue: one student derives *pedantic* from *ped*, 'foot,' and *antic*, 'caper.' *Pedantic* thus becomes 'foot caper,' or 'crazy dancing.' And sometimes the definition is right, but there's still no cigar: *verbose* does indeed mean 'full of words,' but the sentence "The dictionary is verbose" doesn't quite convey the usual sense of the word.

Dictionaries aren't always a help, either. I had a student once who looked up *adulterate* in a pocket dictionary and came up with 'cheapen.' Confident of his now more powerful vocabulary, he forged this sentence: "The teacher adulterated the student in front of the class." On the other hand, that may be exactly how he perceived education. Another student interpreted Shakespeare's image of the beast with two backs, a reference to a human couple in an act of carnality, as referring to a camel.

These colorful near misses have staying power. We may not call chicken salad "Pullet Surprise" at our house, but we'll probably eat bushes, not salads, though I'm keeping the kids away from fern bars for now in case they suddenly decide to get literal.

My Life Is a Charade

I bought a car in the fall of 1990. Some of you may have done the same. I was shopping for price, features, and most of all, reliability. Perhaps the least important thing affecting my decision was the *name* of the car. But Shakespeare placed great store in names: "Who steals my purse steals trash, but who steals from me my good name. . . ." Auto manufacturers, too, see a car's good name as its bond—and perhaps they should, since the name is one of the last parts of a car to go. The auto makers go so far as to register names of cars they may never even make in order to keep other manufacturers from using them. Still, despite their best efforts, not all automobile names are wisely chosen. There is of course the Edsel, named after Edsel Ford, a big shot in the company at the time. The car was a flop, but the name will live on as a symbol of failed enterprise long after we have forgotten more recent busts like the DeLorean. It's a safe bet there'll never be a Chrysler Iacocca or a GM Smith.

Sometimes a car name seems thoroughly ill-fitting. Take the Daihatsu Charade I saw on a street near my office. Now *charade* originally meant 'chatter or babble,' and later came to mean a riddle, first a verbal one, then one which was acted out. A charade is also a deception or travesty, particularly one that is easy to see through. None of this seems designed to sell a car in an English-speaking market (though obviously somebody *did* buy the car). What do you tell your friends? "I'm driving a charade." If your whole life's a charade, you might as well have a car to match.

Then there's the Toyota Cressida. I always wondered about a luxury car whose name, from Greek mythology, is the epitome of the faithless woman. I don't know what the Cressida is called in Japanese, but Toyota's American marketing team must have great faith in our willingness to forget that the name is the last word in unreliability. Or maybe they just assumed Americans to be so culturally illiterate they wouldn't connect the name with the legend. The name of the car I finally bought, the Camry, has no apparent meaning in English—in fact, my Toyota dealer had to call the California headquarters to learn that Camry comes from the Japanese *kamuri*, which means 'crown.' I find that reassuring, but what I like most about the car is that it goes when I turn the key.

Perhaps the best-known story of an automotive language slip is the Chevy Nova. *Nova* is Latin for 'new,' which is a nice enough idea. But Latin is dead. In today's Latin market they speak Spanish, and *no va* in Spanish means 'It doesn't go.' The car did not sell well in Mexico (or at least, so the story goes).

Chevrolet also sells the *Caprice*, which means impulsive or unpredictable change: a capricious car, to me, is one that doesn't always feel like starting. Other names strike me as iffy, too. The *Monte Carlo* suggests 'big gamble' rather than luxury. Is the Hyundai Sonata musical? Not with that little muffler. *Stanza* is a part of a poem, but it comes from Italian 'to stand still,' a sense that the Nissan folks surely hope no one will notice. The Saab Turbo reminds me of a fish, an expensive fish, but still a fish, because of its fish-like name and because it looks like one. The Dodge Shadow follows you instead of taking you with it. And the Mitsubishi Mirage is sheer illusion, a car without substance, something that isn't really there.

Shakespeare also said, "What's in a name? A rose by any other name would smell as sweet." As long as we insist on investing our cars with meaning, why not have cars with flower names? That would combat the image of the car as the great polluter, but it might also reinforce our fears of the greenhouse effect. How about a Mercury Tulip, the perfect car for Spring? Or a Pontiac Snowdrop in February? I'd have to take shots before I could even test drive the Volvo Ragweed, which is deep-discounted in August.

Of course, cars can't always have appropriate names: there are no Mercedes Expensivos or Fiat Fiascos, or are there? And how about the sporty Buick Whiplash? There are cars that evoke the monarchy, including the Monarch, the Regal, the Marquis. Where is the Plymouth Proletarian or the Dodge Capitalist?

The public sees through the funny names of cars. That's why they say Ford means 'Found On Road Dead' or 'Fuel, oil, and repair daily.' Or that the Yugo is aptly named—You go, because it won't. The makers of the Scirocco, a hot, evil wind, might do well not to contemplate a new model called the Monsoon, which suggests a car with radiator problems. And Detroit continues to prefer the El Dorado, the magical city of gold which doesn't exist, to the Model A. Having been to Detroit, I can see why.

The Paleontology of Words

Every once in a while we come across an old word no one ever knew existed. A case in point is the **duck-billed platitude,** a mysterious creature half noun, half mammal, that has recently come to light and is considered to be the ultimate violation of the rules of grammar, as we know them.

Once all we could say about dating a language fossil was, "Only time will tell," but today we have modern, even postmodern, techniques to determine the age of a phrase. For a normal, run-of-the-mill platitude, we go ahead and measure its teeth—if it is a biting phrase. If it is wooden, we cut it open, making sure to use an old saw. Or we split it like an infinitive and count its rings. If it is an old chestnut we roast it, using an open fire, and we can date its ashes fairly accurately using the Carbon-14 process.

Measuring that the duck-billed platitude also poses a new challenge for the grammatical sciences. This paradoxical creature combines features of nouns and mammals in ways that have long puzzled the experts. Like mammals, its young are born live but learn to move by walking on eggshells. However, being nouns as well they can name a person, place or thing at a very young age.

When platitudes roamed the earth.

One hypothesis suggests that the DBP, as it is referred to in the trade, goes back to the paleolithic, or old stone age. That stems from the oft-repeated belief that people who cast stones should not live in glass houses, or perhaps that's *glazed houses,* 'houses with windows.' The fact that the one platitude that has been identified was found buried with a large trove of clichés suggests it may be nothing more than a variation on a figure of speech, an interesting but unproductive sidetrack in the evolution of human language. But more extreme is the suggestion that the duck-billed platitude isn't tropical at all but is rather the result of underground weapons testing.

If so, then this mutant hybrid, which has no natural enemies and has proved indestructible in laboratory tests, could signal what the language critics have long dreaded, an end to English as we know it. Which means I better find that Finnish dictionary after all.

And finally, here's the last question we will have time to answer—
Question: Could you recommend a good grammar book?
Dr. Grammar: Yes. And I wouldn't recommend a bad one. For the name of a reliable language specialist, consult the front pages of your

local dictionary—you know, the pages with the tiny print that nobody ever reads or even uses to press flowers with.

The Unlaws

I do want to leave you with a few observations before the final exam (yes, you heard right, there is a final exam). Sometimes I call these Baron's Laws of Usage, though since usage is so variable, I must warn you that they are likely to change without notice. And since violating them carries no penalty, they are laws without teeth, or even dentures. So I should really call them unlaws.

We saw the first of these unlaws earlier in the book. We may call it *The (Un)Law of Self-Contradictory Inconsistency:*

> Whenever a language critic complains about something you can be sure 1. it's already too late to do anything about it, and 2. the language critic already uses the form he or she is complaining about.

Here are the rest of the (Un)Laws of Usage, at least those unlaws I have discovered up to this point:

The (Un)Law of Uncertainty: When it comes to language, everyone knows the difference between right and wrong, or good and bad, or standard and nonstandard, English, but no two people agree on what that difference is.

The Uncertainty Principle Times Two: Experts disagree over correctness in English even more than everybody else. And they do it louder, too.

The (Un)Law of Everyone's a Critic: For every usage critic watching your grammar, there's another usage critic out there watching his (or her) grammar, and so on ad infinitum, etcetera, and di dah di dah di dah.

The (Un)Law of Don't Tread on Me: Americans want their language to be corrected by the "experts," but they refuse to listen to anything an expert tells them, because they figure, "No one's got the right to tell *me* what to do."

The (Un)Law of, If I'm so Smart, Why Ain't I Rich?: Experts refuse to listen to other experts, because they figure, "No one's got the right to tell *me* what to do."

The (Un)Law of Increasing Entropy: Even if we do try to take a language expert's recommendation about what is correct to heart, we are more than likely to get it wrong and produce yet another error for the experts to get exercised over.

The (Un)Law of Enlightened Self-Interest: Language experts say what they do in such a way as to maximize misinterpretations and get us to make more mistakes so they can stay in business.

The (Un)Law of the Relativity Principle: Everyone's got something to say about the English language, which makes it as hard for the person in the street to distinguish between language fact and language fiction as it is for them to distinguish between science fact and fiction, between history and myth, or between Coke and Pepsi.

The (Un)Law of the Principle of Recurring Punctuation: No matter how often I try to duck the issue and get on to topics that are really interesting, most people still want to know where to put their commas. But that's okay, because, according to

The (Un)Law of the Proper Pronoun: For language, as for anything else, it doesn't matter what you know but who you know. Or is it *whom?*

And now for one last test to see if you've been paying attention.

Final Exam

You've come to the end of the line so far as language repair goes, and it's time once again for, you guessed it, **the final exam.** But I thought, since you didn't have much time to study, that I'd give you a multiple choice questionnaire instead, designed to elicit some of your ideas about English and your guesses as to where it's going. You will notice that this time I don't give you the answers.

Anyway, here's how you do it. From any touch tone phone, just dial 1-800-GRAMMAR and press the appropriate button to register your choice. If the line is busy, or if it's been disconnected, then please write down your answers, using a number-three pencil (if you only have a number-two pencil, sorry, you're out of luck, try the SAT instead).

Ready, now? OK, here goes—

Complete each statement with the most nearly appropriate response.
    1. English spelling reform
       a) would make everyone's life easier.
       b) would make everyone's life more difficult.

c) will make words reasonable and rational and easy to learn, and up to 10 percent shorter as well.
d) will render spelling bees noncompetitive and force more youngsters to consider the Little League alternative.

2. The ever-increasing use of computers by writers
   a) makes writing easier and writers more productive.
   b) adds to the alienation and stratification of society inherent in the capitalist system.
   c) means people will forget how to use pencil and paper.
   d) will expose writers to lethal doses of radiation given off by their computer monitors.

3. The following words or phrases need to be invented.
   a) A word to describe the feeling you get when watching your work disappear from a computer screen never to be seen again.
   b) A word or phrase for a sports event running just a little past the top of the hour so that your favorite prime time soap opera is announced with the phrase, "We now join 'None of My Children are L.A. Lawyers' in progress," which is just another way of telling you you missed the one event on which the entire episode hinges.
   c) A word or phrase to describe the feeling you have when everyone in a group seems to know what's going on except you, and all you can think of is that you must've been absent, but of course you're not in school in the first place so how could that be?
   d) A phrase to use when someone you just met tells you, "I'm an English teacher."

4. The following words or phrases need to be destroyed:
   a) totally awesome, dudes
   b) ya know?
   c) share, as when Julius Caesar said, "I wanna share with you a funny thing that happened to me on the way to the forum."
   d) ain't
   e) grammar

5. Which of these pairs is most nearly opposite?
   a) awesome/awful (Remember, *awful* means 'full of awe.')
   b) dude/dudette
   c) dude/nonturtle
   d) grammar/party

6. If I could have my way with the English language, I would
   a) set up an academy to regulate usage.

    b) limit words to no more than three syllables.
    c) make sure spelling didn't count.
    d) bring back Latin.
    e) ban multiple choice tests. (If you choose this answer it is not necessary to finish the survey.)

7. I use a dictionary
    a) to look up hard words.
    b) to look up dirty words.
    c) to press flowers.
    d) to hide money.

(If your answer is *d* you should know that burglars often use dictionaries to look up hard words or search for pressed flowers. You might want to reconsider your options.)

8. Which of the following statements best describes you?
    a) I frequently correct the language of my friends.
    b) My friends frequently correct my language.
    c) I no longer have any friends.
    d) I haven't spoken to another person for some time.
    e) I would enjoy correcting the language of the language commentator who wrote this. *Whom* should I write to?

All right (that's two words). Time's up. Put your pencils down. Send in your answers to the publisher, and I'll announce them in the next edition of the *Guide to Home Language Repair.* Remember, all teachers defy John Donne's question about who(m) the bell tolls for when they insist that you remain in your seats because "That bell is for me, not for you." Oh, and next time, be sure to bring enough gum for everybody.

Index

Abled, 129
Accent, loss of, 61–62
Advice, free, 10–12
Aerial, 49
Agenda, 28
AIDS, 121, 126
Ain't, 50
Al and I, 108–109
Algeo, John, 121
Already, 26
All right/alright, 26, 60
Alphabet, 7, 24
Ambidextrous, 102
American University of Beirut, 128–129
Anymore, 25
Apartheid, 126
Apostrophe, 37, 40
Arguably, 7
Artificial languages, 73–74
Asiatic, 103
Asterisk, pronunciation of, 33
Austen, Jane, 114
Awesome, 124–125
Axe for ask, 33, 50, 51

Baker, Josephine Turck, 6
Banana, 103
Basics, the, 117–118
Basque, 75
Bennett, William, 54
Berman, Shelley, 132
Bernstein, Theodore, 47
Between you and I, 108–109
Biden, Senator Joe, 82
BIG TIME, 17
Biodegradable, 125
Borge, Victor, 37
Brasserie, 119
Brecht, Bertolt, 84
Brochette, 119
Brown, Goold, 15, 18
Brown, Murphy, 107

Cabasa, 119
Can, 1, 32, 60

Cannibalize, 30
Capitalization, 15
Card-carrying, 123
Carroll, Lewis, 124
Cars, names of, 151–153
Carson, Clayborne, 84, 85, 86, 87
Carter, President Jimmy, 33
Cassideous, 119
Catcher in the Rye, 143
Censorship, 143
-challenged, 129
Channel flippers, 129
Channel surfing, 129
Channel trolling, 129
Chavez, Linda, 105, 106
Chemicals, 126, 145
Children's language, 150–151
Churchill, Winston, 33, 126
Clarke, Arthur C., 123
Cliches, 7, 29
Clinton, Bill, 108–109
Clinton, Hillary, 110
Coconut, 103
Cold fusion, 69, 126
Cold War, 126
Coleridge, Samuel Taylor, 81
College composition, 64–66
Colon, 40
Colorization, 121
Commas
    origins of, 40
    overuse of, 42–43
    where they go, 37–41
Comparative, 17, 20
Competive, 13
Complex sentence, 19
Compound sentence, 19
Computerese, 30
Computer virus, 121
Conjugation, 17–18
Consistency, 28
Copulative verbs, 31
-correct, 129, 130
Correct English, 6
Correctness
    notions of, 5–7
    selling of, 56–57

Couch potato, 122
Creationism, 70–71
Criss Cross, 35
Criterion, 28
Cronkite, Walter, 34

Da, 35
Dacquoise, 114
Dash, 37, 42
Data, 28
Decumbent, 114
Deer, 26–27
de Man, Paul, 105, 106
Derived word, 15
Desert Shield/Desert Storm, 127
Dickinson, Emily, 37, 42
Dictionary(ies), 137–138
　uses for, 8
Dictionary of Modern English Usage, 32
Difficult, 29
Diversity, 62–63
Dolls that write, 66–68
Don'tspeak, 102–104
Dormitory, 104
Downsize, 128
Dribble off, 35
Drown, rule for, 25
Duck-billed platitude, 153–154
Dumpster-diving, 130
Dysphasia, 68

E-Prime, 52–53
Eliot, T. S., 71, 115, 116
English Grammar, 14
English language
　death of, 71–72, 74–76
English teachers
　stereotypes of, 48–49
　training of, 7, 48
Eskimo, 102
Esperanto, 73
Etcetera, 33–34
Ethnic labels, 102
Euphemism, 105, 110, 129
Euro-, 124
Evolution, 70–71
Evolution-challenged, 130
Excellent, 43–44, 125
Extreme, 44

Factoid, 35–36
Facundious, 142
Farther and further, 27
February, 34
Feel bad/badly, 30–31
Fellow, 98–99
Final exam, 156–158
Finnish, 75
First lady, 110–111
Forbivorous, 114
Foreign words in English, 10, 119
Former, 127
Forshuppild, 141
Fowler, Henry, 32
Franklin, Benjamin, 103
Free gifts, 143–144, 145
Fresh ground pepper, 150
-friendly, 129
Frost, Robert, 71

Gardner, John, 81
Gay, 26, 27
Gender-neutrality, 95, 97–98
General semantics, 52
Generation gap, 26
Girls, 101–102
Good-bye, 29
Gould, Edward S., 104
Grammar, test on, 17–21
Grammar abuse, 56–57
Grammar gene, 68–70
Grammar of English Grammars, 15
Green, 125, 126
Green, Richard, 50–51
Greene, Amsel, 150
Greene, Samuel S., 14, 18
Greetings, 29–30
Grutchen, 141
Gusty, 141

Hacienda, 119
Hale, Sarah Josepha, 111
Haley, Alex, 81
Hanged/hung rule, 25
Hard, 29
Harding, Warren G., 82
Have a nice day, 29, 40
Hawaiian, 75–76
Hectic, 26
Hiatus, 126
Hoffman, Abbie, 83

Index

Holmes, Oliver Wendell, 82
Hopefully, 7
Hostage, 128
Humongous, 7

Ice cream, 5
Iced cream, 5
Idiom, 12, 109
Illiterate, 39
Incomparable, 44
In-depth summary, 144
International language, 72–74
International Society for General Semantics, 52
Intertriginous, 114
Inuit, 102
Iron curtain, 125, 126

Jefferson, Thomas, 87
Jeopardize, 104
Johnson, Samuel, 137
Journal, 26, 104
Joyce, James, 143
Junta, 7

Kakonis, Tom, 35
Kazantzakis, Nikos, 143
Keating, H. R. F., 40
Kempt, 141
Kennedy, Jack, 82
Kielbasa, 119
Kilometer, 7
King, Martin Luther, Jr., 84–87
Korzybski, Count Alfred, 52

Labels, 102
Lady, 110
Lady Chatterly's Lover, 143
Laloplegia, 114
Language and patriotism, 61–62
Language police, 47–63
Last Temptation of Christ, The, 143
Latin, 28, 71–72
Lawrence, D. H., 143
Lawyers, 25
Lehrer, Tom, 91
Leniency, 104
Less/fewer rule, 23–24
Liberal, 122–123, 124

Liberry for library, 33
Like/as, 20, 28
Limacine, 119
Liquor, 27
Literacy crisis, 148
Literary clothing, 148–149
Lloyd, Charles Allen, 61
Longman Guide to Good Usage, 59–60

Mailer, Norman, 35
Maitre, H. Joachim, 85
Majorly, 17
Make My Day, 45–46
Malapropisms, 69
Mallon, Thomas, 81, 85, 90, 91
May, 1, 32, 60
Mazagran, 119
McCarthy, Senator Joe, 105, 123
Meat, 147
Mega, 17
Melville, Herman, 146
Merriam-Webster, 121
Meshummad, 119
Microwaveable, 122, 124
Middle English, 141
Miller, Keith, 86
Mistake, 104
Morigeration, 119
Morpheme, 15
Mother of all, 127
Ms., 59–60, 98
Mucho, 17
Multiple personality disorder, 88–89
Music, 146–148

NASA, 76–77
National Homework Test, 78–80
Natural popcorn, 144, 145
Nemoral, 119
Nephelometer, 114
Newspaporial, 114
Nixon, Richard, 123
Noetic, 130
Nootropics, 130
Nuclear, pronunciation of, 33
Number of, a, 11–12
Numnah, 114
Nunberg, Geoffrey, 52

Obscenity, 101

Octarchy, 119
Oreo, 103
Oriental, 103
Orthography, 14
Orwell, George, 5, 52
Outplacement, 128

Parasol effect, 130
Parenting, 27
Parker, Dorothy, 82
Parsing, 19–20
Passive voice, 5, 20, 52, 59
Patient, 30
Peace dividend, 126
Perfect, 44
Period, 40
Phalacrosis, 120
Phenomenon, 28
Phonemes, 14
Phone words, 132–135
Photographic-memory gambit, 88
Physicist, 5
Physicsist, 5
Plagiarism, 81–94
    double standard in, 84–87
    excuses for, 88–89
    by professionals, 89–91
Plumbeous, 119
Plungers, 130
Plurals, 11
Police words, 130
Political correctness, 101–102, 104–106
Political Dictionary, 123
Porter, James, 87
Portnoy's Complaint, 143
Post, 127
Post-empty nest family, 128
Postmodernism, 121
Pot, 26
Potatoe, 107–108
Pourboire, 119
Precision, loss of, 27
Predicate, 19
Preferred customers, 145–146
Preposition
    defined, 32
    ending sentence with, 31–32
Presidental, 5
Presidentess, 111
Presidential, 5
Primitive, 15
Procacity, 114

Pronouns, declination, 17
Pronunciation, 33–34, 56
Punctuation, 37–41

Quarter of, a, 6
Quarter till, 6
Quarter to, a, 6
Quayle, Dan, 106–108
Quindlen, Anna, 110
Quotation marks, 39

Radical, 15
Reason . . . is because, the, 72
Relevant, 64
Reliable, 5
Rely–on–able, 5
Rightsize, 128
Romania, 7, 24
Romany, 24
Roots, 81
Roth, Philip, 143
Roumania, 7
Rumania, 7, 24
Rushdie, Salman, 142

Sacciform, 114
Safire, William, 35, 47, 123
Salami, 119
Salesman, 3
Salinger, J. D., 143
Satanic Verses, The, 142
Scientialist, 5
Scientist, 5
Second-person plural, 96–98
Semantics, 147
Sentence diagrams, 8
Sentences
    defined, 18
    essential elements of, 18–19
    simple, compound, complex, 19
Server, 99–100
Sex-neutralization in language, 95, 97–98
Shakespeare, William, 28, 44, 92, 109, 114, 122
Shall, 27, 60
Shock radio, 22, 122
Simple sentence, 19
Slave printer, 30
Smart drugs, 130

Smiley face, 40–41
Solresol, 73
Sontag, Susan, 121
Sounds in the English language, 5, 14–15
Soupet, 141
Soviet Union, 60, 127
Spelling, 14, 16, 112–120
Spelling bee
    French, 115–116
    value of, 113–115, 118–120
Spelling checkers, 114, 116–118
Spenser, Edmund, 7
Spoonerisms, 69
Standardized tests, 79–80, 92
Steal This Book, 83
Stentorophonic, 114
Sterne, Laurence, 81
Stevenson, Adlai, 123
Stolen Words, 81
Subject, 19
Subject-verb agreement, 20
Such as, 28
Suffragette/suffragist, 95–96
Superlative, 17, 20
Swarthy, 103
Syllable, 15
Synopsis, 17

Taboos, 101–102
Taft, Senator Robert, 123
Tauromachy, 120
Teaching English, 64–80
Telegram, 5
Telegrapheme, 5
Televisual, 9
Ten don'ts of English, 9–10
Tessaraglot, 119
Test(s), 13–26, 79–80, 92
Textual appropriation, 86
That, 18, 27
Thurber, James, 42
Tip surfing, 130
Tough, 135–137
Trademarks, 131–132
Tristam Shandy, 81
Trudeau, Gary, 102
Turner, Ted, 121, 122
2001, 123

Ulysses, 143
Unique, 44
United States Postal Service, 41–42
Universal language, 72–74
Usage, Baron's Rules of, 6, 155–156
Usage guides, 59–60
Used-to-be, 127

Vanity phone numbers, 132–135
Very excellent, 43–44
Video grazing, 129
Vidiot, 129
Vizetelly, Frank, 6
Vocabulary building, 58

Wait, 99–100
Waitperson, 99–100
Waitri, 99–100
Waitron, 99–100
Walkman, 131
Wannabe, 127
Webster's, 131, 137
Weltpolitik, 119
Whatcha doin', 50
Which, 18, 27
White, Richard Grant, 47
Who, 27–28
Whom, 27–28
Wilde, Oscar, 136–137
Will, 27, 60
Words, power of, 142–143
Word surfing, 129

Y'all, 97
Years with Ross, The, 42
You betcha, 50, 51
You guys, 97–98
You know, 100–101
Youse, 50, 51, 97
You'uns, 96–97

Zoo, 138–140
Zorba the Greek, 143

Author

Photo Credit: Bill Wiegand/University of Illinois

Dennis Baron is professor of English and linguistics and director of first-year composition at the University of Illinois at Urbana–Champaign. He has written and taught about language reform and attitudes toward the English language for twenty years. In addition to having taught high school English, directing summer writing workshops for teachers, creating radio programs about language, his background includes membership in NCTE's Commission on Language. A former Fulbright fellow at the University of Poitiers, France, he has held fellowships from the University of Illinois Center for Advanced Study and the National Endowment for the Humanities.

His books include *Grammar and Good Taste: Reforming the American Language* (Yale University Press, 1982), *Grammar and Gender* (Yale, 1986), and *The English Only Question: An Official Language for Americans?* (Yale, 1990). *Declining Grammar and Other Essays on the English Vocabulary* was published by NCTE in 1989. Although committed to high seriousness and the academic life, he has recently begun to dabble as well in the fine art of cartooning. In addition to their publication as illustrations for the *Guide to Home Language Repair,* his cartoons have appeared in *The Chronicle of Higher Education.*